CONFESSIONS OF A CHINA-HAND

CONFESSIONS OF
A CHINA-HAND

BY

RONALD FARQUHARSON

LONDON
HODDER AND STOUGHTON

First printed 1950

MADE AND PRINTED IN GREAT BRITAIN
FOR HODDER AND STOUGHTON LIMITED
LONDON, BY C. TINLING AND CO., LTD.
LIVERPOOL, LONDON AND PRESCOT

For BUNTY
and
The Twins

CONTENTS

		PAGE
I.	Herr Hao	11
II.	Mai Yeo Fa'tze	34
III.	Face	49
IV.	Manchuriana	61
V.	The Attaché Case	73
VI.	Journey with Jason Ho	90
VII.	Ah Fat	100
VIII.	Tally Ho	116
IX.	Shanghailander	128
X.	Travel-Amah	139
XI.	The Hill	152
XII.	Portrait of a War Lord	162
XIII.	Return to Eden	193

AUTHOR'S FOREWORD

IN offering to the public these stories of incidents so largely concerned with my personal activities in North China during an earlier decade, I would like them to be accompanied by a word or two both in explanation and acknowledgement.

With the exception of "THE HILL", which is a fantasy in actual surroundings and somewhat different from the others, the incidents in themselves are recorded very much in the manner of their actual happening. It is natural, perhaps, that I have considered it expedient in certain instances to substitute names and in others to alter localities or sequences. I have deliberately added adjustment and a little colour to my "PORTRAIT OF A WAR LORD" in order that he may emerge with the best characteristics among three whom I knew and, though I have no doubt that many of my contemporaries in China will recognise him despite it, it might be unwise—even at this date—to make him more widely apparent. "RETURN TO EDEN" is very much a personal story; so personal in fact that I have deliberately cloaked it with another, losing my true identity in both: and some, I hope may read it who were also my companions on the famous Kikungshan train in the summer of 1926; they, of course, will know the reason why.

As for the others, I think they may be offered without further comment.

I am proud to acknowledge the fact that a few among the happenings recorded in these "CONFESSIONS" have already made their appearance in *Blackwood's Magazine;* and I am particularly grateful to Mr. G. D. Blackwood for the encouragement which he thereby extended to a new and unknown spare-time scribe.

My final word is one of affection for the Chinese, particularly those whom I met and knew during my travels through the remoter regions of their country; quite a few among whom figure in the pages of this book and are—need I say it—real characters. To each of them, whether they yet survive, or already be journeying towards "The Yellow Springs" I owe and acknowledge my deepest debt of all.

RONALD FARQUHARSON.

THE GRANGE,
  WETHERAL,
    CUMBERLAND.

November 21st, 1949.

I

HERR HAO

HOPING to create the impression of a young man determined to lose no time in justifying his appointment to a commercial post abroad, I had presented myself to the Sales Manager of our organisation in China within an hour of my first setting foot on the Shanghai bund. I discovered him a preoccupied person possessed of an imperial liver who shot me a disparaging glance, rebuked me for arriving on mail-day and forthwith despatched me to the native city in a ricksha. There, greatly aided by Mr. Yee, who had accompanied me from the office, I immediately proceeded to prove my prowess by disposing of a case of cod-liver oil to a Chinese Apothecary who normally dealt only in native herbs. Mr. Yee, however, insisted that this early opportunity must be taken of extending "Face" to the newly arrived Englishman; and the Apothecary, boasting a single tooth of startling prominence and the equally odd and appropriate name of Mr. Fang, expressed himself as willing to comply on the understanding that if, thereby, be extended "Face" to a twenty-one-year old Foreign Devil, he, in turn, must be extended twenty-one days credit.

On such agreement and the promise of immediate delivery, Mr. Yee and I bowed ourselves backwards out of the premises into our rickshas. Of this incident it only remains to relate that twenty days later, as might well be anticipated, the case of cod-liver oil was mysteriously translated from Mr. Fang's shop back into our Godown.

During the intervening period I had entered my proper apprenticeship in the simpler aspects of the Chinese Commercial Art, and "Face" was preserved through my having disposed of a modicum of merchandise in a more genuine market. Nevertheless Mr. Yee continued to exploit his same expedient whenever newcomers arrived from England, one can only suppose, in the rather vain hope that on some such occasion the face-extending Mr. Fang might, prior to the expiry of his credit, forget to return the goods.

Shortly I was packed off to a Northern outpost where my modest attempts to introduce and foster British trade, chiefly among the merchants and farmers of a nigh-limitless *hinterland*, assumed a richer, far more fascinating aspect than was ever confined within a homing case of cod-liver oil.

·   ·   ·   ·   ·   ·

There were established native industries, invariably of a crude and primitive nature, to be discovered in the scattered and far-distant cities and *hsiens* which, with the aid of our technicians, we aimed to encourage and develop, the better, we hoped, for the prosperity of Chinese and British alike. There was new ground to be broken in the less accessible, unexplored, territories which lay close to Mongolia in the North and stretched out towards Turkestan and Tibet in the West: here we assayed to open up trade in an unchanging world that was oblivious to the march of a thousand years.

And over all lay the soil,—so much of its pristine richness spent
through centuries of crude cultivation—that once good earth
of China, from the slender fruits of which countless millions
took their pittance, or, in the unyielding years, perforce must
perish: we sought, through small beginnings, to nourish that
soil, to enliven it with the scientific discoveries of a modern
era, thereby to strengthen the slender thread by which vast
communities lived or died. It was essentially Trade; but
brightened by humane purpose: I, with the ardent ideals
common to Youth, interpreted it as Commerce with a Cause
and, at intervals, trekked out into the Unknown mentally
panoplied as though on a Crusade. It was a propitious state
of mind, for in the 20's and early 30's there was little else in
favour of forsaking the easy club comforts of a Treaty port
for long weeks of hard and hazardous journeying through
uncharted wilds where, blown by winds from the Gobi, only
the grey dust danced for one along age-old solitary ways.
And after the rains the dust made mud: such mud as men
have only trod in Flanders' fields, or—say—on the devious
track that travellers take to reach Yangchu.

Yangchu, more familiarly known by its pre-Republic name
of Taiyuanfu, is (or was) the capital city of Shansi province.
During the days of which I write, all communications including the dilapidated railway which spasmodically ran
North and South through the province, were only permitted
to function in the interests, and at the dictates, of the local
War-Lords. This indeed was the era when only bribery was
brother to belligerency in the control of provincial affairs:
under such conditions of corruption and chaos none but the
sorely-tried and over-taxed merchants strove to maintain that

high standard of honesty which is inherent in the character of their kind.

On the proverbial assumption that it was better to travel hopefully than to arrive, Mr. Kim and I approached Yangchu, overland from the East, ensconced in a springless ox-drawn cart. After a full week's earlier journeying from Tientsin across the plains of Chihli, we had now travelled a further five days, jolting our precarious way along a hundred and fifty miles of scarcely discernible track from Changtingfu in the adjoining province now known as Hopei, where we had done good business. But we were now faced with a more formidable task; for we had learnt that our German competitors had established in Yangchu a native Agent called Mr. Hao who was obviously far more progressive and resourceful than our own representative. Mr. Hao had apparently contrived to overcome the existing obstacles of transport and distribution with the result that stocks of the German product had poured in and were flooding the whole of Shansi. We, on the other hand, had not so much as a picul throughout the province. While this was to the extreme detriment of British business, it was also a state of affairs with an even more aggravating aspect; it was *we* who over the earlier seasons had broken the ground and almost our hearts in the process; it was we who had staged the experiments; we who had first nourished the earth and sown the seeds that waxed as magic to incredulous eyes: all this we had done before a competitive *chop* had even been designed. And now, through some artifice as yet unknown, it seemed that the Boche rode home with the harvest. The object that lay immediately ahead of us was no more than to discover the answer to one question: the Spring was far spent now; the season had been lost in Shansi; we must know how the Germans had won it:—that was all. With that knowledge, we might plan a campaign even better than theirs and recapture the province next year. But how to glean the secrets of Mr. Hao? He would not be delivering them as a gratuitous gesture to any who asked; most assuredly he would hold them more precious with the ears of the enemy around. Our problem was one of approach—for probe those secrets we must.

One of the wheels struck a boulder embedded deep in the mire and we lurched suddenly to one side, causing my head to come into violent contact with the bamboo stay across which curved the blue cloth cover of our primitive cart To Mr. Kim's consternation, the blood trickled down from my temple: but I waved aside his ministrations, for the jolt had dislodged a dormant idea.

"Kim," I cried, "I have it! It's come to me at last! This fellow Hao," I went on, "I've no doubt he's progressive; maybe somewhat of a wizard in his way; but he's more than likely to be a local lad who wouldn't know a Highlander from a Hun."

"So what?" drawled Mr. Kim, a Chinese born in Honolulu who had subsequently graduated in Agriculture at an American University.

"Just this," I explained, "suppose we breeze straight into *Herr* Hao and introduce ourselves as being a couple of the *Farben* freaks on a routine round: you know, same as we do with our own Agents; checking up stocks, surveying the market, finding out about this and that—the usual rigmarole: he'd be none the wiser while *we* most certainly would."

"You mean—we'd learn the 'know-how'?"

"Exactly. All's fair . . . isn't it?"

Mr Kim ruminated for a while and then to minimise the risk of losing either in the act of speech, secured his last bit of Spearmint to a loose stopping and at length remarked:

"Guess so. So long as there are no genuine Huns in Town."

I calculated the odds against such a possibility to be remote: the Germans were no fools and, with the sowing season over in a locality that bristled with fireworks, nobody but inquisitive fools like us would venture about a volcano.

"Little chance of that," I said: then added, "incidentally there's just one thing."

"What's that?"

"You'll have to do the lying for me: I don't know enough of the lingo yet."

Mr. Kim leant forward on his haunches and then looked back at me with a growing expression of horror:

"Jeez!" he exclaimed, " now if I were British, I'd say you had a bloody face!"

I put the best construction I could on his remark and dabbed at my head with a wad of disinfectant.

. . . . . .

Mr. Hao steamed his spectacles above a bowl of tea, wiped the lenses clear on the wide sleeve of his gown and, having replaced them about his nose, proceeded to regard us across a red lacquered table with an evident degree of benevolence. He was a rotund, middle-aged son of Shansi, surrounded by an atmosphere that betokened both prosperity and importance. Mr. Kim, with a dead pan expression on his features, had duly intimated our identity to Mr. Hao as being akin to his, in that we were adherents to the agricultural interests of the Fatherland. He achieved this, however, not without difficulty, since his Chinese conversation was an odd mixture of Mandarin and Cantonese, a combination of dialect which was entirely unaided by the addition of a strong American accent: nevertheless it appeared to prove sufficiently effective as to cast no shadows of doubt over the beaming countenance and spontaneous welcome of our seemingly unsuspicious host.

During the course of the subsequent exchanges I was able to comprehend the substance of much that was said by Mr. Hao, since he spoke slowly in the same measured tones which were invariably employed by my native teacher in Tientsin. I formed the impression of his being both scholarly and astute, a learned live-wire; but over-all a kindly and a courteous man, with such an obvious abundance of charm that I became increasingly conscious of a growing distaste for my presence before him as an impostor. But it was too late for withdrawal now; I could do no more than regard my personal reactions as attributable to weak-mindedness and endeavour to overcome them by silent self-assurance that the objects of our mission were too vital for considerations of sentiment. But I still found difficulty in convincing myself that we were here to outwit the Germans and that Mr. Hao was no more than a means to an end.

Without the necessity of obvious questioning, the factor which lay behind the overwhelming success of our competitors in Shansi soon became abundantly clear. Their Agent was a man of wide influence who cultivated the right people in the interests of his business. Unlimited quantities of the German product had been transported into the province under the umbrella of "Military supplies", by means of the commandeered railway running South from Kalgan. In the recognised order of things, there was little doubt that Mr. Hao subscribed handsomely to the local War Lord's coffers in return for the privileges of this monopoly; but, even were it an expense not recognised by the Germans, it was an investment which, with now only obscure prospects of British competition in the future, would ultimately continue to reap for him ever increasing dividends.

"If the earth declines to yield a harvest," explained our host, "then a million piculs of rice must be imported into the province, by the military, in order that the soldiers of Shansi will not starve. It is wiser, I think, to assure the harvest; and that is why supplies of your product become a military necessity."

This utterance, said with all that emphasis of sincerity which the Chinese language commands, appeared so logical as to outweigh the considerations of bribery having entered into the arrangement and, in my mind, Mr. Hao immediately assumed the added stature of a statesman. He had now told us all that we wished to know, which made it seem obvious that, short of appointing the Military Governor of the province to act as our Agent, we might as well under present conditions, write Shansi off the map. I concluded that we had better be proceeding on our way to peddle our wares elsewhere; but since Mr. Hao appeared so amicably disposed towards us, the elementary courtesies demanded that our stay be prolonged, at least until our host had been allowed some opportunity of giving further expression to matters which he regarded as being of moment.

"I am," he was saying, "no more than a humble native of a troubled province in the centre of a civilisation that crumbles and decays through sheer antiquity. It is good," he went on, now regarding me steadily, "that the science and culture of the great German nation should contribute to the reconstruction of our worn out way of life, and I am honoured only less in my unworthy association with your great Industry, than I am by the privilege of your presence in my humble surroundings.'

Mr. Hao bowed elegantly in my direction and then took a sip from his bowl of tea which he imbibed with an audible degree of relish. I glanced across at the faintly amused expression on Mr. Kim's face and, having finished my own tea, could accomplish no more than a slightly parched swallow. With a rasping noise, our host cleared his throat and went on:

"It is good that this victory in commerce should have been won over a country who some years ago cheated you out of victory in war. It is but a beginning: the wise ones say that shortly a man may rise from obscurity among your people and that through his inspiration your arms, too, will be all victorious and that within a decade you will conquer England."

There was a deep and deathly silence, during which it seemed that Mr. Hao was expecting me to confirm or deny the intuitions of his wise ones; but I felt that it was better to remain dumb than to risk betraying any sense of my discomfort. It was Mr. Kim who broke the rather tense atmosphere by saying, with an exaggerated air of cheerful indifference.

"So the product is selling well?"

The Agent turned to face my companion, who was nervously chewing on his remaining particle of gum, and replied in the briefest possible terms:

19

"No."

Mr. Kim stopped chewing and his jaw dropped open.

"No?"

"The quality is poor," said Mr. Hao.

The incredulous Kim repeated the first syllable of the Chinese expression for "poor" but the act of framing it caught him unawares and caused the gum to shoot from his mouth across the table where it lodged on the side of Mr. Hao's tea bowl.

Quite oblivious to this slight domestic tragedy, the Agent went blandly on:

"I have acquired samples from competitive sources and though the selling price does not differ, my experiments show that the substance does. I think you must improve the quality of your product, for it is indeed far inferior to that of your enemies the British."

I observed Mr. Kim anxiously regarding the now somewhat embellished pattern on the tea-bowl across the table; but I knew his perplexed expression was more attributable to the fact that he was as well aware as I was that the analysis and quality of the German product never varied and was, moreover, identical with that of the British make.

"Nevertheless," continued Mr. Hao, who now rose and drew open the drawer of a chest behind his chair, "since there are no stocks of the higher grade commodity in the Province, I have managed to dispose of no more than a paltry nine thousand piculs; and, again, since the disturbed conditions prevent me from relying on the postal service, I trust you will excuse me for asking you to accept personally my draft for sixty-eight thousand dollars in settlement."

Never before, nor I am glad to say since, have I been called upon to accomplish such a feat of fast thinking. But as I struggled to explain that travelling with such a sum on my person would be no more than inviting the unwelcome attentions of bandits, I was interrupted by an alarming sound which emanated from the region of Mr. Kim's epiglottis, and it did not surprise me in the least to learn that, in the maelstrom of these unexpected developments, he had now succeeded in swallowing his loose stopping.

"Very well," concluded Mr. Hao, as with extravagant courtesy he bowed us back to our waiting cart, "I will bring the remittance with me when I travel to your honourable Treaty port within the third moon from now, and thus allow myself the humble privilege of acknowledging the distinction of your call upon me to-day." He bowed twice. "So—until the seventh moon—safe journeys to you both."

My companion and I were some distance on the long trek home before we found that words once more came easily to us.

.   .   .   .   .   .

Surrounded by easy comforts, some two weeks later I sat within the solid security of the British Concession in Tientsin, and, for the edification of my Directors in Shanghai, proceeded to compile a chapter concerned with my recent life-history. When this self-styled masterpiece-among-travelogues came to touch upon the unhappy state of our affairs in Shansi province, any erstwhile qualms of conscience concerning Mr. Hao had entirely forsaken me; and I permitted an extravagant eloquence free rein to dwell at length upon the artful subterfuge which I had so successfully adopted, in the Company's interests, at Yangchu. The task completed, I relaxed even more deeply into a blissful state of self-satisfaction, visualising, at delicious intervals, the nods of approval and the expressions of appraisal which the report would hardly fail to evoke round the Board Room table. I was impatient only for the acknowledgement which most assuredly would manifest an adequate degree of recognition for services so resourcefully rendered.

I had not long to wait: a several-page epistle arrived for me by return mail.

Since the close of our contemporary days in the Far East, I am still frequently fortunate enough to run across the one-time Director of our China Company who dictated that letter before signing it with a discernible degree of emphasis about his familiar flourish. In mellowed maturity he politely professes to have forgotten the incident and I take delight in reminding him of certain expressions which he rightly considered appropriate to the occasion. Indeed, those expressions—like the remarks contained in one of my earlier School reports on Chemistry—("might do better if he desisted from playing with every tap, bottle and drawer within reach")—remain indelibly implanted on my mind, despite the tumultuous years that have intervened:

"I must now refer to that lengthy section of your report wherein it is stated that you unhappily chose to represent yourself as belonging to the German Organisation, in order to elicit certain information from a native Agent. Any value which might be attached to your discussions in Yangchu must be discounted entirely through the harm which will inevitably result from such an ill-considered action. What will be Mr. Hao's opinion of you and what will be his impression of the Company which *does* employ you, when he learns of your true identity? I must point out most emphatically that this is not the manner in which our Company would wish to go about its business. British Commerce in China has been built up on unerring principles of absolute honesty of approach and undertaking . . ." and so it went on, *ad lib;* there were pages of it!

Subconsciously, I suppose, at the time, but more realistically later on, I appreciated the full worth of the man who wrote me that letter; he was grand and he was genuine: and, moreover, every word of it was so absolutely right. I read it through but once; then hurriedly stuffing it into my pocket, I took a ricksha round to the Club where, aided by the ministrations of the bar boy, I proceeded to peruse it many times more. Then I relapsed into an easy chair and started to consider the implications of the whole thing.

Some few hours later I emerged—a man of action—upon the world again; and if there was a slight suggestion of unsteadiness about my gait, this was amply countered by the firmness of my resolve. First I sought out my native Teacher and emphatically declined to be parted from him until he had succeeded in imprinting, for all time, upon my memory the means of expressing in Chinese—"Good morning. I am not German, I am your British competitor. I offer my most humble apologies for having deceived you. May your offspring remain forever fertile. I must now return. Good-bye." Next, I lost little time in completing arrangements for an absence of at least a month; and in the afternoon of the same day, before my impulses were allowed the chance to become discouraged through considerations of foolhardiness, I was on my way. I was going back to see Mr. Hao again, in far-away Yangchu; and this time I must needs make the journey alone.

．　．　．　．　．　．

The hunchback who owned the inn at Showyanghsien kept no calendar to relieve the monotonous mud walls of the sanctuary which I had shared with a variety of resident vermin and where I had continually held court to a colony of neighbouring rats. But, as I took my departure, I calculated that we must be approaching the sixth moon, that I would have lain here for over a week and, if not yet free from fever, I should at least, by now be immune from the attentions of the armed and grizzly horde who had so long persisted in their endeavours to track me down.

Except during the period when I had been spasmodically delirious, unsought circumstances had granted me ample opportunity for reflection: dysentery, especially when aided by a touch of the sun, was a depressing malady, no doubt adding weight to the volume of my self-recrimination. I realised that my plight was primarily due to the fact that, over a month ago, I had risen from an easy chair in the Tientsin Club on no more than a starry-eyed impulse. Even after that, following recovery of a more balanced sense of values, indication was not lacking as to the direction in which lay the wiser ways of discretion. The flood-swept city of Hokienfu, with its promise of more perilous paths ahead, should have sufficed to soften the hard core of my stupidity. But little credit can accrue to a persistent fool who deliberately blinds himself to risks for which, should calamity come about, his unsuspecting and innocent employers would be called upon to accept a large measure of responsibility. It would have served me justly if, for instance, in the quite likely event of my capture by bandits, my Directors flatly declined to bail me out: but, of course, they would feel reluctantly obliged to pay the price of my ransom, which would indeed be many times higher than all my potential worth. Yet despite such inescapable considerations, I continued to persist along indiscernable mud-submerged tracks, more stubborn, more deserving by far of its cruel fate, than my companionable mule which slithered whimpering to eternity in a six-foot depth of mire: its last despairing look of helplessness was to haunt and sicken me on subsequent and more solitary days, during which I, perforce, must proceed on foot.

Even in retrospect it comes more easily to gloss over the almost unbelievable difficulties into which my sheer pig-headedness was to lead me. Lack of food, stagnant water, sweeping rains followed by damp humidity and a scorching sun, inadequate ability to seek and understand guidance, with the inevitable discovery that one had wandered a hundred miles off course: these were a few of the hazards to be met in the tracks of that treacherous mud. They were sufficient in themselves to place me on familiar terms with gnawing hunger and heartbreaking, unsheltered loneliness: they gave me a knowledge of how it feels to be stricken with sickness when one is alone and utterly lost, far beyond the limits of habitation. There seemed such little advantage in it all at the time, though in later days one appreciates the wealth of philosophy that is born of precarious plight. If my dire discomforts were no lasting cure for dogmatism, at least they left me with these legacies: in after

years a tolerance to times which seemed exacting; the certainty
that ever to despair is to dally no less than with disaster; and,
most comforting of all, the knowledge that a sense of fear
becomes strangely allayed in the realisation that relief lies
beyond the power of personal action. Indeed, in such circumstances, one becomes most conscious of human frailty and its
utter dependence upon sublime and simple Faith; such, indeed,
as that which brought me through the more merciless miles of
mud, to meet again with Mr. Hao.

．　．　．　．　．　．　．

Mr. Hao sat bolt upright at his red-lacquered table as though
he were a figure hewn from stone. If his features betrayed any
sign of emotion as he took stock of the unkempt creature that
stood before him, then it was no more than one of mild surprise.

My mission was of brief and specific purpose and, having
greeted him in Chinese, I proceeded to the simple task which I
had journeyed so desperately over great distances to fulfil.

"*Wo pu shur Ter-kuo jen: wo shur Ying-kuo . . .*" I began and
thus continued until my apologia concluded with a slight bow
and I half-turned to take my leave and embark immediately
upon the uncertainties of a long trek home.

But, as I was turning from him, I observed that an unexpected change had overcome the mien of Mr. Hao: whereas he had
listened in polite and solemn stillness to my address, a measure
of animation now swept across his features as he stretched forward an arm to indicate the dragon-gilded chair which was
placed opposite to him across the table. It was as though some
graven image had come to life, maturing as an unemotional

enigma who, for no more than an unmasked moment was, none the less, unmistakably moved.

"I thank you." He paused perceptibly. "Now—please, sit down."

Instinctively I obeyed, since physically, and to a certain degree mentally, I was utterly exhausted. Then my sluggish mind stirred me abruptly to my feet again and I looked keenly across at the man who had spoken. He now wore a tolerant smile such as might become some ancient sage from whom no secrets of the heart and mind are hid.

"You would appear," he went on, "to be a little surprised."

"I didn't . . ." I stammered. "I never thought . . . that . . . I didn't realise that you spoke English."

As I sat down again Mr. Hao inclined his head slightly forward and regarded me rather gravely over the horn rims of his spectacles.

"It is not easy," he remarked, "for one who speaks only Chinese to obtain a degree in one of your English universities."

"No . . ." I observed, in an ill attempt to conceal my bewilderment. No—I suppose not. But last time, when . . . when . . ."

"When you were a German?" suggested Mr. Hao blandly. "Perhaps then it would have appeared discourteous to address you in English."

I was given time to consider the implications and aptness of this remark whilst two bowls of piping hot tea were placed on the table before us. Simultaneously we removed the saucer-like tops and bent our heads to sip from the steaming fragrance.

"Mr. Hao," I began presently. "You may not have under-

stood . . . I have come to offer my most humble apology.
I . . ."

With a deft twist which shook it free from the deep folds of
his sleeve, my host raised an elegant hand:

"Your Chinese was excellent," he interjected, "but it was
unnecessary, for I am quite unworthy of your remarks."

Then, as though to subscribe a greater degree of emphasis
to his words, he leant towards me across the table and went
on, "But as an honourable gesture I shall always treasure it as
the greatest courtesy which I have ever received from a
foreigner."

That was sufficient for me. Now, for the first time in five
doubtful weeks, a warm glow of gratification enveloped my
whole being, leaving me singularly refreshed in the assurance
that his words had adequately justified my purpose and that,
after all, I had not plodded on, through tortuous days, to no
avail.

"When I received word that you were coming," continued
Mr. Hao, "I despatched a request to the Garrison Commander
at Pintingchow to furnish you with a bodyguard, so as to
ensure your safe passage from the Provincial borders to
Yangchu."

As he paused to take a further sip from the bowl before
him, I leant back in my dragon-gilded chair, utterly dumb-
founded by the fact that any knowledge of my journey should
have reached him. But I knew that to give tongue to my
curiosity would be discourteous and probably prove no more
than a vain attempt to probe the unaccountable art of Chinese
Intelligence, which foreigners will for ever fail to comprehend.
Presently he proceeded serenely on.

"It was known that you had crossed into Shansi east of Chengtingfu and were seen to be approaching Showyanghsien. But after that, all trace of your movements was lost: the Garrison escort had searched some days, before presuming, to my dismay, that you had perished along the road."

Maybe I might have been forgiven an audible sigh as my hands moved along the arm rests to clutch at Imperial claws and I sank back into bitter, unavoidably ironic, reflection. I found no heart to inform such a solicitous friend of the extent to which I had employed my meagre resources in order to achieve sanctuary from the armed rabble I had steadfastly believed to be a fearsome horde of marauding bandits. In retrospect, how frequently have I smiled rather grimly at the thought of the heavily-bribed hunchback at Showyanghsien turning them twice away from within feet of where I lay.

"I must express apology," Mr. Hao droned on, "for my discourtesy in not meeting you personally at the borders of the Province in order to allay the natural suspicions which no doubt caused you to take refuge from my ill-considered attempts at succour. But it was essential that I visit Kalgan . . ."

"Mr. Hao," I felt that at all costs I must interrupt him by some expression of appreciation. "It was kind of you: I never thought . . . You see . . . I . . ."

Then I realised how hopeless and inadequate any attempts at explanation would appear and I felt gratified when, after a polite pause, he took up the threads again.

". . . it was essential that I visit Kalgan before I could proceed in my negotiations with *you*."

"With *me!*"

As the tea bowls were being replenished I tried to think of

any matter which he could possibly wish to negotiate with interests against which he had so successfully competed. Then, after loudly clearing his throat Mr. Hao proceeded by degrees to enlighten me.

"On the occasion of your earlier visit, I addressed you and Mr. Kim in terms which I thought to be in keeping with the identity which you chose to adopt—for which courtesy I hope that you will now grant me pardon."

He paused, while we gracefully bowed in each other's direction and then went on:

"But when I spoke about the poor quality of the German product, I trusted that you would take notice of the fact—if indeed you were not already aware of it."

"Aware of it!" I protested, "I am only aware of this—that the quality of the German product is identical with that of our own. We have an agreement concerning quality, as well as price, to which both sides faithfully adhere."

Mr. Hao regarded me gravely, as he had done earlier, over the tops of his lenses.

"You still do not know, then, that the German cargo has been deliberately and persistently adulterated?"

"Adulterated!" I exclaimed. "Who has been adulterating it?"

Mr. Hao did not answer: inscrutably, he did no more than continue to regard me over the rims of his spectacles.

It suddenly dawned on me that, for some reason, Mr. Hao had been under the impression that, even if we had no direct hand in it, my Company must be aware that some nefarious influence had been at work to discredit the quality of the German product in Shansi. I was naturally intrigued to learn more.

30

"Where has this happened?" I persisted.

"At Kalgan," replied Mr. Hao. "My stocks come by way of Kalgan where they are delayed until such time as I can arrange with the military to take delivery by rail at Tatungfu in the North of the Province. You see," he went on, "it is well arranged: adulteration has taken place after the goods have passed beyond German supervision but before I become accountable for them. It means of course," he concluded, "that the Germans must accept responsibility."

"And what . . . what have you done about it?" I enquired.

"I have withdrawn all the remaining stocks throughout the Province," replied Mr. Hao, "and since the farmers have now lost confidence in your competitor's product, I have undertaken to replace each bag next spring with the British commodity."

I found it difficult to contain my immediate excitement over this quite unexpected development, until, to some extent, it was to be dispelled by certain obvious complications.

"Mr. Hao, you must be aware that nothing," I repeated the word to lend it emphasis, "*nothing* could please me, or my Company, better: it is unfortunate only that no German Agent is considered eligible to deal in the British product."

"It is unfortunate only, perhaps, for the Germans," replied the Agent, "in that they must take the responsibility if the cargo of which I take delivery at Tatungfu is largely composed of sand and chalk. My monetary losses are of little account: consideration, though of my 'Face' is paramount. I have accordingly notified the German principals that I am no longer able to act as their Agent."

"Ah! This was better," I thought. There only remained the

31

consideration of our own Agent in Yangchu whom I had not yet visited: perhaps it would be possible to bring him and Mr. Hao together in partnership: that might be one solution at least.

"The question of our already established Agent in the Provincial capital worries me," I said. "While he is by no means a man of your merit and distinction, I know of no wrong he has done such as might call for cancellation of his agreement with us."

"No," said Mr. Hao, sombrely, after a long pause.

Then he rose a little abruptly signifying that our discussions on the matter were at an end and in brighter tones begged that I be his guest, that I would eat at his table and rest for two days in his house after which he would personally escort me back to Tientsin, under military influences, by rail.

"The journey," he concluded, "should take no more than thirty-six hours."

.   .   .   .

"Hell's a'poppin'," remarked Mr. Kim.

"Is it indeed!" I observed. "What have I done wrong now?"

"You go twice to Yangchu," replied Mr. Kim, "and never check up on our own Agent."

"Well . . ." I glanced across my desk at the imperturbable figure of Mr. Hao gazing impassively out of the window at an assortment of native craft steadily plying the Pei-ho. I turned back to Mr. Kim.

"I did call. He was away. They told me he was in . . ." I stopped abruptly. Then, "What is the trouble, exactly?" I enquired.

32

"The Huns are mad as hell," supplied Mr. Kim. "They've called on our Directors about the adulteration of their stocks in Kalgan."

"But . . . but has that anything to do with our Agent in Yangchu?"

Mr. Kim's reply was abrupt and to the point.

"Seems like—*everything*."

"Everything!" It confirmed a suspicion that had only just dawned on me in the recollection that, when I had called upon him, they had said that our Agent was still absent "on business" north of the Shansi border. And as the full significance of so much seeped in upon me, I glanced across once more at the inscrutable Mr. Hao.

With half-closed eyes he appeared to be following intently the smooth passage of a white sail which was moving majestically alongside the approaches to our Godown.

"I was considering," he said presently, with a full degree of deliberation, "considering that in the coming spring we should employ the clear canvases of many inland water craft to advertise, with due elegance, the supreme excellence of our mutual commodity."

. . . . . .

II

MAI YEO FA'TZE

Mai yeo ku'tze, mai yeo wa'tze,
Mai yeo chi'en:—mai yeo fa'tze.

No trousers, no socks,
No money:—no matter.
(Mandarin jingle)

A FAMILIAR Blue Funnel towers above the saucy turbulence
of attendant tugs; rope leads are hurled, with the accompaniment of a salty oath, towards the quay: and in the fullness
of time, following rigid adherence to the intricacies of immigration, one who has wandered about the Northern Cities and
unexplored bye-ways of now-distant Cathay is once more
afforded access to the sweeter soil of his native shore.

But after the first vain efforts to find adjustment within the
tempo of renewed existence in what is gladly accepted, in its
essentials, to be a never-changing England, one becomes
resigned to continued classification as a Foreigner. Only
gradually does the returned, but as yet unrehabilitated, exile
begin to attract that cautious, half-attentive, measure of
interest which makes itself manifest by the casual, often ill-conceived, questions of an aggravatingly insular mind. Variable
only in its degree of disregard for distances, comes the earliest
and the inevitable:

34

"Been in China, have you? Then you must know a bloke called Brown in Bangkok."

One politely points out that he was probably before one's time, whilst restraining an impulse to air the more appropriate response in reference to "a chap called Charles in Colombo."

But what has really inspired this brief memoir is the recollection of a question that was directed at me by a fair "Modern" across a luncheon-table in Mayfair. In precise terms it went like this:

"But *do* tell me: how on earth did you cope with those *frightfully* fantastic hieroglyphics which they scrawl backwards —or something: without *actually* qualifying for certification, I mean—or *did* you?"

The way she put it took a bit of sorting out, but I considered it sufficient to reply briefly to the effect that I disdained to "cope" which was presumably why I was still permitted to roam at large! The same query, however, though perhaps couched in less enigmatic terms, has persisted down the years, which suggests that certain light reflections concerned with the Foreigner's approach to the calligraphy and conversation of the Manchus may possibly serve to sustain a modicum of interest.

In actual fact, unless one was "Diplomatic", "Consular", "Maritime Customs", or no more than an ultra-studious adherent to Commerce with an insatiable thirst for unusual knowledge, one was wise assiduously to avoid any serious exploration into the limitless field of Chinese characters. That is, of course, apart from the more familiar ones which it pays to recognise on the face of Mah Jongg tiles and those which may appeal to the cynically-minded as being particularly apt: such, for instance, as the one—beloved of Ben Travers—which depicts two women under one roof, and means—quite simply —"Discord". No one knows exactly how many thousands of years ago it was that the ancient artists of China first started transcribing their thoughts into pictures, but who shall deny that their wisdom must be of like antiquity!

Neither, I believe, is it known exactly how many thousands of these intricate and carefully chosen signs exist, since I have always understood that not one among the great Celestial Scholars has ever acquired a knowledge of them all. The educated native man-of-business rubs along quite nicely on well under a thousand, whilst, I have been told, most official documents can be de coded with a recognition of no more than five hundred. During ten years in China I eventually succeeded in recognising, all told, about twenty of them; and with a masterly flourish of the brush could create a fair representation of less than a dozen: three of these comprised my name, and three more the brief style of the Company which employed me (these six being invaluable for the purpose of obtaining native credit) and then my calligraphy tailed off into portraying the numerals one to three, which a sidelong glance would detect as being no more than their Roman counterparts assuming a horizontal attitude. A pretty poor performance on the whole, maybe; but, if I may be permitted to say so, richly compensated by what I, at least, believe to be a continuing state of sanity: a condition possibly different from that current in certain stark-eyed Student-Interpreters whom I used to observe mouthing Manchu monosyllables and sketching strange signs in the air about the Legation quarter in Peking.

Unless, therefore, the necessity is paramount, or the urge

beyond control; to the Westerner, who, whilst retaining respect for the balance of his mind, aspires to read and write in Chinese, my advice, for what it may be worth, is quite simple: let him be content to read this—it's far easier—and write the other ambition off! *But* I would add that to understand, and particularly to talk, the spoken idiom of Mandarin is a glorious experience and well worth the minor effort its acquisition entails. It is fascinating study and a vastly different bowl of tea to any straw-in-the-hair excursions into hieroglyphics. It is a language which is lyrical and full of music; it is rich in charm and subtlety of expression; furthermore, being entirely devoid of grammar, its assimilation avoids recapturing, for many, what must often have been the despairing atmosphere of the Fourth Form room in an era of earlier struggle.

But of course there are pitfalls. The inevitable one is immediate failure to appreciate the fact that there are four distinct tones employed in the enunciation of each syllable and an incorrect intonation is frequently apt to convey quite the wrong meaning which, on occasions, has been known to introduce an unexpected and somewhat startling element into the most prosaic conversation. The sound *"p'ing"*, for instance, according to character and the intonation it is afforded, can give expression to matters so widely diverse as a block of ice, a military gentleman, or the distressing circumstances of *mal-de mer*. Again, the word *"mai"* uttered in one tone can be interpreted as "to buy" and in another, only a shade different, it means "to sell"; whereby it may be seen that a knowledge of intonation cannot wholly be disregarded. But once over the fence, the going is dead easy for one merely has to combine "to buy" and "to sell" together—in a word *"mai-mai"* and that means "business". "Simple as poo-ding!" to use an expression once employed by my Chinese teacher.

Lest it be thought at this stage that I am usurping the functions adequately catered for by the School of Oriental Languages, with an unsteady excursion into the phonetics of Peking, let me quickly lead on to (and then even more hurriedly pass on from) the unhappy experience of a stately lady who, professing a deep but too distant interest in the Far East, journeyed out to China for a sojourn of eight weeks, during which period she assayed to absorb the ancient customs, the sublime atmosphere, and the rich tongue of the forgotten Manchu dynasties. She was the widow of a highly successful citizen of the United States, perhaps somewhat more kindly than cultured, and she had obviously allowed an extreme degree of earnestness to subdue any evidence that she was possessed of a sense of humour. I must admit that she acquired quite a lot of things during her stay in Peking: but they were more material than aesthetic and consisted mainly of unwieldy and horribly grotesque *objets d'art* which, even if they had, as she proudly but erroneously proclaimed, emerged from the Forbidden City, would certainly be equally forbidden in any home or museum which retained even the milder elements of taste and refinement. I suppose that the truly gullible can buy more appalling rubbish in Peking than anywhere else in the world, and she certainly must have garnered a rich harvest for the bowing bazaar-boys of Morrison Street.

It must be said in her favour, however, that she was never lacking in self confidence and, having successfully angled herself an invitation to dine at the British Embassy, found the courage to inform the grave-faced Chinese official who was

seated next to her, that she had acquired a good working knowledge of his tongue. I can vouch for what followed, since I, too,
had successfully angled myself a similar invitation, and, with a
feeling that I would, if necessary, have gladly trekked across
the Gobi desert in order to be present at what might ensue, I
composed myself as calmly as possible on her other side. As I
anticipated, following her remark, the grave-faced Chinese
official, whose air was the epitome of dignity and his manners
as elegant as the pattern of his long blue gown, took her at her
word, and, bowing gracefully, proceeded to address a series of
remarks to her in the slow, soft-falling lilt of the true Mandarin.
She half-turned from me and gave him her full attention; but
it was only too obvious from the very start that she was
hopelessly out of her depth. But still the Official, seemingly
oblivious to the fact, droned on, employing all the stops and
delicately touching the pedals that lent timely and beautifully
interspersed variety to the melodious tones of his recital. Here
was a genius even among a race of masters in the art of richly
enhancing the spoken word: just to listen to his voice was
music to me: but to the lady for whom he fashioned his
exquisite phrases—even *that* was obviously lost on her. I
hesitated before wading in to her assistance: I hesitated, and
then it was too late. She had said it!

The first time she said "*Shur*" the polite official blenched but
slightly, swallowed sharply and then, concluding that his ears
must have deceived him, continued his peroration as though
quite unmoved. Then a moment or two later, having
rounded off a long and particularly elegant phrase, he was in
the act of restoring some much required wind to a pair of
depleted bellows, when she said it again. This time he glanced

sharply at her and there was a perceptible quickening in his intake of breath as his jaw hung momentarily open. Then, as if to purge himself of some dark thought quite out of keeping with his sense of elegance, he shook his head and, leaning slightly more towards his by now quite hopelessly confused audience, proceeded manfully on . . .

"*Shur*" expressed in the appropriate tone, can be translated as "Yes", or, to amplify it, as "Yes—go on—this is very interesting" which, although she had not understood a solitary word of what the Official with the melodious voice had been saying to her, was precisely the expression which the American woman, who foolishly professed to know Mandarin, had intended to convey to him. Indeed, what a mountain of difference can be created by the slightest error in tone!

Then she muttered "*Shur*" on the incorrect, and embarrassingly lower, note yet again: and, as though she were a drowning woman, went down for the third and last time, never, I profoundly hope, again to breast the tide of Chinese conversation without a better knowledge of its most essential feature. The Chinese Official drew back, suffered a slight, but opportune, spasm known as the restrained choke, and then graciously turned his grave countenance in the other direction. *He* was not to let her know and *I*, on whom she was subsequently obliged to depend for the rest of her dinner-time exchanges, lacked the courage to apprise her of the *gaffe* she had so innocently perpetrated. But I would dearly have loved to do so, supposing there had readily come to my mind some delicate means whereby I could explain to a lady the precise expression that "*Shur*", uttered in the tone which she had employed, conveys to a Chinese.

I smile secretly and enjoy the reflection of that incident, not for a moment at the expense of the unfortunate woman who probably never gave the matter another thought: no, though the English of the expression which she unwittingly used might be tolerated in quite respectable company confined to men, it just intrigues me to reflect to whom it was passed and where. Verily, there is no person to be found possessed of a greater sense of dignity than a Manchu Official of the old school; and I presume that, apart from the interior of a Cathedral, there is no atmosphere more hallowed than that surrounding an official dinner at a British Embassy.

.   .   .   .   .   .

From the earliest days of my arrival in North China, I was taught something of the four tones of Mandarin by a native professor of great antiquity whom I can best describe as being a man of shapes. His figure was fashioned in the form of a question mark, his inch-long finger nails after the manner of talons, while his carpet-slippered feet stood permanently at a quarter to three. His voice reverberated like peals of thunder rolling across the Western Hills and he was known by succeeding generations of his pupils as "Roaring George". His knowledge of English never appeared to extend beyond such expressions as "Wrong-tone", "Same-meaning", and "Again-pliss", supplemented by a few rather alarming phrases which I suspect were taught him in moments of levity by young Britons who had retained something of their school-boy exuberance.

His practice was to arrive at my house at eight o'clock in

the morning, immediately proceeding upstairs to my bedroom where the lesson began: in due course he would follow after me, still roaring in my wake, to the bathroom where he drooped over me, seemingly from a great height, as I performed my ablutions: he continued to bellow at me from all sides as I dressed, and finished off by draping himself opposite me at breakfast, the conclusion of which coincided with that of the day's learning.

If, as more frequently was the case, I had been riding for an hour before "Roaring George's" stentorian tones greeted me from halfway upstairs, I was in a fairly receptive state of mind; if I had forgone my exercise I was only moderate: and if there had been a party lasting into the small hours, my four tones were apt to reflect the state of my liver and had a tendency to be somewhat more than sluggish. On one occasion—I think it must have coincided with a Naval visit—I crept up to bed no more than a hundred minutes before the professor himself was due to mount the stairs, no doubt to regale me with his usual greeting of "*Hao-pu-hao*" (literally "good-no-good", meaning "are you well or otherwise?"). But "Roaring George", bearing down upon me as I lay in the uttermost depths of oblivious slumber, had to choose that particular occasion to work off on me one of the slightly crude phrases which he had accepted from some poker-faced young Englishman as the most solicitous enquiry into one's state of health usually adopted at Court.

"How . . ." he roared from directly above me. "How—is—your—Lordship's—belly—for—spots?"

No untimely cannonade beneath my bed would have served to shoot me into a bolt upright position with a greater degree of alacrity. "Could I *possibly* have heard him aright?" One hand went automatically to my head and the other clutched feverishly at the pillows in mortal terror and bitter anguish that I should have "got 'em" after such a brief and really quite restrained career of drinking. There was only one other occasion when that same fear of having to share my existence with strange phenomena assailed me: and that was on awaking one Christmas morning to find three turkeys perching in drowsy line along the bed rail below me: but that was before I realised that, in the matter of poultry, the Chinese always "bring 'em back alive".

But, for the moment, there was "Roaring George", having delivered himself of his astounding utterance, hovering about in the half-light like a genie emerging from the bottle, to float presently towards the window where his talons clutched at the curtains. Even in my half-conscious state I sensed there was more of this nightmare to come:—and come it did!

"Do I," he bawled, "now—un-cork—the—day-light?"

"No!" I hurled back at him, "you do not! *Kwei-kwei t'so* (quick quick go) and chase your Aunt Fanny round the race-course!"

I hardly thought he would succeed in memorising that one: but it was sufficient to me for the moment that he was able to grasp its portent: and he hurriedly disappeared out of my life until the next day when, I am glad to say I was feeling more *hao* than *pu hao* and he, in turn, was content to confine his remarks once more to "Wrong-tone", "Same-meaning" and "Again-pliss".

Except for these expressions supplemented on rare occasions by the somewhat eccentric phrases which I have quoted (and a few others concerning which it would be better for me to maintain a discreet silence) "Roaring George" had no English vocabulary: neither did he favour the use of a dictionary. But he overcame what would otherwise have been an obvious handicap, particularly with raw recruits, by truly remarkable displays of histrionic ability. He could cry like a child, crow like a rooster, contort himself into the shape of almost anything and treat me to vivid impersonations of a steam engine at speed or a water buffalo bellowing to its mate. His act of illustrating what was meant by the Chinese word "to expire", which he staged, with a wealth of diminishing groans and gurgles, followed by a long period of complete inertia, on the bed I had just vacated, was so realistic that it was not without some feeling of relief that I subsequently witnessed him arising from the dead.

In many ways lovable though he was, I concluded that "Roaring George" was, for me at all events, rather more of an entertainment than an adept in the art of pedagogy: but lacking the heart to substitute him, I eventually decided that a prolonged tour of my district in the Interior might do more for me than merely serve to rectify a financial condition that was beginning to show an alarming tendency towards expenditure over income.

I had come to Paotingfu and simultaneously to the conclusion that, short of resort to murder, it would be easier to run away from the inseparable companionship of a devoted greyhound than to persuade the Office Interpreter to allow me to proceed on my travels without him. I understood that we had agreed to part company at two earlier points on the journey: and on each occasion I had trekked confidently along on my own in a

Peking cart fifty miles or so across the wastes to the next town or village, only to discover my companion patiently waiting for me in our Agent's shop. I never found the courage to ask him how he had contrived to travel at such high velocity in a wellnigh trackless country, since I have always maintained a terror of the supernatural and would sooner stumble across an up-to-date dinosaur than be shown a carpet actually possessed of magic qualities. I could fathom it out no further than that. But at Paotingfu providence did me a better turn than that which it meted out to my fast-moving interpreter. He fell into an open cess-pool and broke his leg.

I stayed with him for a week and then consigning him to the medical care of a Scottish missionary, I set out to continue the still formidable schedule of widely scattered visits that lay ahead, accompanied only by a wall-eyed charioteer who was obviously less capable of expressing his sentiments than were the ill-bred brace of mules behind which we jogged and jostled together for days on end.

For the first week I must confess that I had some bitter regrets about my rashness, for I found that the going was truly tough: but it is remarkable how quickly one's senses can combine, *in extremis,* to frame an appropriate appeal for the urgent necessities of life—sustenance and shelter,—or in seeking out the way. After a fortnight I had doubled my Chinese vocabulary but what was more, I felt instinctively that the timbre of my tones was improving as well. At the end of three weeks I discovered that I could sustain a single conversation relating to business matters with my Agents for a full minute without recourse to "*Wo pu ming-pi*" ("Me no savvy") every ten seconds.

By the time I had picked up my interpreter again at Paotingfu I had developed such cracking form that I was able to memorise a long but unfamiliar expression he employed to the wall-eyed muleteer and lost no time in trying it out in its entirety immediately upon renewing my acquaintanceship with "Roaring George". It certainly proved to be a Roland for his Oliver for, on hearing it, the Professor's eyebrows shot up so high that they appeared to lose themselves somewhere in the region of the button that nestled upon the centre of his cap: which was perhaps hardly surprising since, as I was subsequently to learn, I had succeeded in casting the gravest doubts on the authenticity of his ancestry over a period of six generations!

.   .   .   .   .

So it was that I came to know, despite a wealth of differing local dialect, that the soft tones of Mandarin will see the traveller successfully through all but the Southernmost provinces where they indulge that comparatively tuneless tongue—so full of its *kwoks and kwaks*—that is known as Cantonese.

But the two women under one roof; the peasant with a bundle of sticks; the small boy with the fishing line; the half-open gates; and the square pierced by a shaft of sun which is the character for China itself: all these and the remaining multitude of mosaics in miniature are common throughout the length and breadth of a once-wide Empire ruled, down the dynasties, from the Dragon throne in Peking. Actually, they extend further: for though through the centuries they have suffered a sea-change, the origin of the hieroglyphics adopted by the subjects of the Mikado, claiming direct descent from

Divinity, can be clearly traced to Influences which sought no more than to be considered collectively Celestial.

. . . .

In anti-climax, may I add that in a remote corner of the province now known as Hopei I once happened across a Bavarian who was unsuccessfully endeavouring to deal in fire-extinguishers solely on the basis of practical demonstration backed up by a few phrases of pidgin English. With a proper degree of deference, I suggested to him that if, for reasons of his own, he was averse to the employment of a qualified inter-preter, he might well proceed to further economies in acts of petty arson succeeded by expenditure of chemical squirt, through acquiring, without undue difficulty, a working know-ledge of the common tongue more appropriate to his wide market. In a sense, I suppose, he answered for far too many miscellaneous commercial emigrants from every country in Europe and beyond, who regularly head towards the East and aspire to trade with the honest merchants of China.

"Ach!" he exclaimed. "Before to China coming, it is neces-sary only the English to learn."

Some years later, I relayed the portent of this exchange to a prominent official at the Ministry of Industry and Commerce in Nanking. It brought forth an impatient gesture accompanied by the expression *"mai yeo fa'tze"*. Literally it means "without fashion" and more often than not in the English idiom, it suggests "no matter", or "it is of little account". In other words, the official at the Ministry intended to convey that if such were the methods through which the Foreigner sought

47

to do business in China, he, personally, couldn't care less.

Then again, an American, professing to have become bi-lingual within a fortnight, had his own interpretation of the same expression.

"What it means," he drawled, "is that it's kinda screwy."

So it will be seen, indeed, that all things are not necessarily alike to all men and, by the same token, you, personally, are at liberty to label this as you will. However that may be, I am well content to let it rest at—*Mai yeo fa'tze.*

.   .   .   .

III

"FACE"

Aʟᴛʜᴏᴜɢʜ in all I only spent comparatively brief periods during my employment by a large Industrial concern in North China travelling through the Interior, it was on those occasions that I learnt almost as much as any Britisher can of the language and customs of the Chinese Merchant. If this was so I claim no credit, for the most hopeless dullard could not have been the student and fellow traveller of Mr. Ho without becoming fascinated by his appreciation of the native outlook and the elegant approach of his philosophical mind to meet the intricacies of all occasions. As a mentor he was supreme, for one never tired of learning from him. As a business asset his worth was incalculable, though no spoken praise nor more material reward would ever persuade him to be conscious of the fact. He would not, for instance, accept the credit for one of his most impressive achievements in collecting a debt of thirty-eight thousand dollars which one of our up-country agents—a certain Mr. Tsao—had owed my Company for a very long time. Mr. Ho's generous loyalty almost convinced me that I had some share in the honours but in actual fact I merely played to the best of my limited ability the minor role in which his inexhaustible patience had previously rehearsed me to near perfection.

The facts of the case are interesting for they serve as an

example of the reactions of an honest Chinese, unimpressed by the manners of the West, to any approach that is not accompanied by the age-old courtesies which personal prestige, or, more briefly "Face" demands. Two earlier visits by members of our English staff, unaccompanied by Mr. Ho, had completely failed to impress upon Mr. Tsao the urgency of a settlement. They reported a conviction that he was bankrupt. In the meantime business in the area of Hopei Province under this agent's control was being sadly held up and my object now was to make a last effort to collect the debt or, alternatively, take preliminary steps towards appointing a new representative. Thirty-eight thousand dollars, even in Chinese currency, was a lot of money in those days, but it was of less importance than the urgency of maintaining and expanding British trade against threatening competition from other sources.

The long journey from the then treaty port of Tientsin to Mr. Tsao's headquarters had, for the most part, been undertaken by native cart and during the four days and nights we had spent en route, Mr. Ho had not only vastly improved my knowledge of his tongue by politely ignoring any remarks which I passed to him in English, but had also contrived to create within me a state of mind more likely to be receptive to the atmosphere of the approaching exchanges.

Now the stage was set and the curtain had already risen on a dimly lit room which smelt strongly of kerosene and was overstocked with many crude and strangely assorted pieces of furniture. As I looked across the table, it was difficult to discern the blunt features of Mr. Tsao, but obviously he was giving polite ear to the rambling discourse of Mr. Ho. In the melodious, richly emphasised tones of the Northern dialect, my companion held our host's attention by leading from one topic to another—all quite remote from the object of our visit, the real nature of which would be quite obvious to Mr. Tsao.

Occasionally one or other of us would take a sip from the bowl of tea before us. It was piping hot but seemed little more than water touched by some exotic flower-like fragrance. At intervals the three bowls were replenished by a very small and earnest-faced young boy to whom it would appear that extra-vagant courtesies were no more than second nature. Mr. Ho, whose hands, like those of the agent, were firmly embedded within the sleeves of his gown, was now approaching the height of his eloquence, relying only on the intonation of his voice to impart colour where emphasis was demanded. Mr. Tsao's features became less impassive as he turned from the speaker to me and back again to indulge a child-like interest in a graphic description of the perils of Shanghai traffic on Nan-king Road. To a man of fifty or so, who had never travelled beyond a ten-mile radius of his own compound, the sight of a motor car would have been a complete novelty. It was doubtful if he had even seen a bicycle. Long before Mr. Ho had begun to spellbind our host with further tales of modern invention, Mr. Tsao had exclaimed "*Ai Ya!* (Goodness me!) what will the foreign devils be up to next". But if his terminology was ill chosen, the remark was innocently and kindly meant.

Then, most unexpectedly, Mr. Tsao suddenly changed the whole nature of these pleasantries by introducing the subject of one of our chief products which had become an essential commodity to the local community.

"My stocks are exhausted. I shall require a further three

thousand piculs before the rivers close," he observed non-chalantly. "What is the price Ho Sien-seng?" (Mr. Ho).

"But Tsao Sien-seng," protested Mr. Ho. "You are aware that it is our practice to send you this cargo on consignment terms. That means we do not expect you to pay for it until you, in turn, have sold it. Certainly it will be our duty and pleasure to despatch you a further three thousand piculs and would ask in immediate return no more than that you should advance us the shipping charges as usual."

There was a prolonged silence, broken eventually by the slightly perplexed tones of Mr. Tsao.

"As usual?" he exclaimed. "Such a request I have never before heard. It would not be possible for me to consider losing Face to the extent of advancing shipping charges. What thing is this, Ho Sien-seng?"

Mr. Ho half rose in his seat and bobbed his head at the pouting features of the Agent.

"I humbly beg ten thousand pardons of you, Tsao Sien-seng, that we did not make you previously aware of this new regulation of our Company. Let me explain that many hundreds of li away, where our humble Company has an Agent far less illustrious than your honourable self, it happened that a considerable cargo was ordered and shipped at great cost when there was but little water within the river beds. After the waning of three moons, that considerable cargo returned at the expense of our quite unworthy Company to the point from which its mighty journey had originally begun. Some devil, it seems, had entered the market of that obscure Trader and devoured the buyers of our quite unworthy wares. Our humble taipans were extremely wroth and set forth the unhappy decree that all agents should henceforth be humiliated by advancing the charges for shipping. The Lords of Fa Sienseng and myself must feel themselves protected."

At the introduction of my name Mr. Tsao directed his now bewildered gaze towards me.

"Such a thing may be," he protested, "but you would not ask the humble yet honest Tsao . . ."

The rest of his sentence was lost as Mr. Ho quickly played his ace.

"Fa Sien-seng, no less than I and all our Lords and Taipans, knows but too well that you, the most honourable Tsao, should have been deemed the one and everlasting exception to this degrading decree, but after much consultation we considered that were an exception made of our greatest and most worthy Agent, he himself might come to take it amiss. Who knows but that such action might not be interpreted as a suggestion that it was a financial impossibility for him to meet this new obligation. Indeed it hurt us to contemplate the considerable Face of which we might deprive the honourable Tsao were we to suggest excluding him from the arrangement."

Mr. Tsao considered this for a long time whilst on his normally expressionless features could just be distinguished the glow of Face preserved.

"How much," he eventually asked with an air of resignation, "would the shipping charges be on three thousand piculs?"

Mr. Ho reached for an abacus from the table and with a few flourishes of the fingers went through the process of making some rapid calculations. He then turned his imperturbable gaze to the smoking kerosene lamp and answered blandly. "Thirty-eight thousand, one hundred and twenty-three dollars and fifty cents."

"*Ai Ya!*" exclaimed Mr. Tsao, in a somewhat stricken voice. "*Ai Ya!*" Then his whole countenance lit up with a broad grin. The significance of it all had dawned on him and the humour of it pleased him, even though the joke was against himself. Then he assumed an air of mock seriousness.

"Thirty-eight thousand, one hundred and twenty-three dollars and *how* many cents?" he enquired.

"Fifty," replied Mr. Ho briskly, with a small bow.

Then the three of us joined together in uproarious laughter at the thought of such exactitude.

As the merriment died down, the entire subject was considered closed as Mr. Tsao entered into the most abject apologies for the rudeness of his humble surroundings and suggested that we might care to accompany him to an utterly unworthy restaurant in the neighbourhood where a few common dishes might be made available. There would be the added inducement of a sing-song girl to entertain us, though we should have to excuse him if we considered the whole meagre offering to be little more than fit for bandits.

Mr. Ho's reply to this display of extreme mediocrity was to bestow upon Mr. Tsao the titles of high degree, then relapse into ecstasies over the grandeur of his house and the obvious elegance of his ancestry. He rounded off this dissertation with a few remarks concerning the over-generous hospitality he was extending to two unworthy strangers whose presence could not but lower their host's prestige in the district and cost him considerable face among his less exalted neighbours. This battle of wits to see how wide the social scale could be stretched between two students of the courtesies continued until we reached the restaurant. By that time Mr. Tsao had degraded himself to the rank of ignorant peasant presuming to walk in the company of a potentate. But a few minutes later Mr. Ho had assumed the role of disreputable beggar demurring to seat himself at the same table as a chief official and merchant prince combined. I felt this was another round in favour of my companion and only hoped that when my turn came, as it inevitably would, that I should do him justice.

The meal provided by Mr. Tsao was a veritable banquet. In a confusion of disorder came the plates of sliced pork, delectable soup, eggs that were black from long burial, sweet puddings, beef balls, chopped liver and much more besides with intermittent appearances of steaming towels to wipe the brow and hands. Throughout all this Mr. Tsao officiated with innumerable kettles of hot *samshu* which served to warm one to a better appreciation of the proceedings.

By the time the bowls of rice arrived to indicate the termination of this orgy of eating the discomfort of my stomach was hardly less than that of the fingers of my right hand which were numb and cramped through two hours' continual association with chop sticks. These minor aches however were nothing compared with the periodic torment of the finer senses occasioned by the entertainment of the local artistes. In a corner of the room sat a very old and somewhat nonchalant musician who spasmodically drew forth from a two-stringed fiddle a series of nerve-shattering discords. From time to time his efforts were supplemented by the performance of two flashily-dressed and rather frightened-looking little girls who warbled high-pitched and, to me, quite tuneless ditties. The lyrics in each case, appropriately enough, concerned themselves with sad tales of those who had languished long before finally expiring in excruciating agony. Perhaps Mr. Ho really did like it, but I fancy not quite to the extent he praised the whole exhibition to Mr. Tsao for the benefit of all concerned.

Then we were joined by two of our Agent's acquaintances who were introduced to my companion and me with a great display of ceremony. After much bowing and shaking of one's own hands towards all and sundry, and the formalities of exchanging cards, the new arrivals divested themselves of a quantity of clothing and settled down very much at their ease. One of them, Mr. Kwo, suggested that the party might shortly repair to his unworthy home and smoke a pipe or two of his inferior opium. But the other, Mr. Ouyang, was of the opinion that it would be better to call for the Mah Jongg tiles and play a game for mild stakes in the restaurant. This was eventually agreed upon and after a considerable exhibition of politeness and much demur all round they eventually accepted from me what I hope was a courteous refusal to participate in the required four.

I sat and watched them awhile and although hardly a word was exchanged it was obvious that a considerable amount of money was passing from the direction of Mr. Tsao. I realised with dismay what was obviously becoming of the Company's dues but not without sorrow, for I found in this recalcitrant Agent much that was easily lovable. Gradually I became less and less conscious of the rapid monotonous click of the tiles and the impassive features of the four contestants, as utter weariness from long travel and much eating could no longer be denied.

It was after midnight when Mr. Ho woke me to say that the game was at an end and then to add quietly, for obvious reasons in English, that Mr. Tsao had lost nearly two thousand dollars.

My immediate reaction was to exclaim *"Ai Ya!"* As I gathered consciousness again, I saw that our visitors were preparing to depart and that our Agent was in the act of producing from his person a further quantity of notes with which to settle the bill for dinner. He appeared in not the slightest degree perturbed by his reverses and on the way home chatted gaily to Mr. Ho about the possibilities of selling perhaps a further thousand piculs of the Company's products over and above what he had previously predicted as being his requirements for the next few months.

As the heavily-barred doors to the Agent's home were thrown open by a weary-eyed watchman, Mr. Tsao remarked indifferently:

"The shipping charges are very high of course."

"But," replied the ever-ready Mr. Ho, "soon perhaps the long and eagerly awaited waters will flow through the river beds towards our undistinguished treaty-port of Tientsin: and then," he paused for a moment, "and then, Tsao Sien-seng, how much reduced those charges may be."

"Must the rivers be in full spate," enquired Mr. Tsao, "before the boats can bring my cargo up?"

"I think in full spate, Tsao Sien-seng."

We had settled ourselves once more in the dimly-lit room with the smoking kerosene lamp above us when I was con-

scious that the agent was regarding me closely and I knew that
he was about to give the cue to say my piece.

He addressed me in slow and distinct Mandarin.

"Fa Sien-seng: you are an Englishman?"

"I am indeed an unworthy foreigner from England," I
replied.

"But you speak the Chinese language very well indeed."

"You are generous and kind, Tsao Sien-seng, but it is true
that I speak but a few words. I fear my ignorance is profound."

"Fa Sien-seng, you are not only a big man with strong
arms, but I think you have a great and a good heart too."

I caught Mr. Ho's eye and he nodded approval. I gathered
that in his view Mr. Tsao was not just flattering to deceive.

"We Chinese that are away from the treaty-ports do not
understand the language nor the ways of the Foreigner,"
continued the Agent, "but we recognise those who appreciate
the elegancies which it is our custom to observe. You are
such a man, Fa Sien-seng, with a good heart and it is deserving
that you be given 'Face'.   I will give you this 'Face' that may
serve you well when you return to the Great Taipans who
make such laws as their protection demands."

I did not fully comprehend the significance of this last address
for it was out of text among the many variations of possible
exchange in which Mr. Ho had so patiently schooled me.

I hesitated for a moment and foundered. But Mr. Tsao
continued on a different tack as though my confusion had
quite escaped his attention.

"Fa Sien-seng, you are the third foreign man who has
come to me from your distinguished treaty-port this year.
Those others: they neither understood the language nor the

courtesies in which you excel. They spoke indifferently one sentence which was without the fundamental of refinement. It may be that your honourable lords who desire protection have suggested those same words to you. But I have not heard you utter them nor do I think that it will be so. Those others: they would not lodge in my humble house, nor partake of my poor offerings of common food. Neither would they accept one bowl of my poor quality tea. They spoke only of money—though it is true that it is the money of your Company. You are wiser than they, Fa Sien-seng, for you are not unmindful that 'Face' is the first courtesy and you have preserved an elegance that I would not lose even for the sake of immediately honouring a due obligation."

I thanked him in terms which employed the majority of the flowery expressions and courteous phrases which Mr. Ho had taught me, and I had succeeded in memorising a great number of them. Not only did I feel that the occasion was appropriate, but I found myself giving tongue to them in all sincerity though it is probable that much of my speech was lost on Mr. Tsao through my inability to lend proper distinction to the four varying tones of the Northern Dialect. The effort was obviously equally exhausting to the three of us, for it brought the curtain down on the proceedings for the night as we parted on terms of mutual and more than ordinary admiration.

As I retired to bed I felt there was much that it might benefit the Westerner to learn from the more genuine people of a nation that was at the height of its civilisation at the time of the Norman Conquest, and who, away from the influence of the Foreigners, had changed but little in a thousand years. I wondered, too, if in a country where the factor of time is of such little account, our mission to Mr. Tsao was to end in success. I earnestly hoped it might for, though he would undoubtedly repudiate them, Mr. Ho was deserving of laurels.

· · · · ·

Shortly after dawn we had taken our farewells from the Agent and Mr. Ho and I were firmly ensconced in a native cart surrounded by our various belongings. Through an aperture in the blue covering of the vehicle, Mr. Tsao, in the manner of an afterthought, was addressing some last words to us.

"My servant," he said, "has included in your luggage some quite unworthy porcelains of an old dynasty. Their value, as you may see, is but a few tens of dollars each but your acceptance of them as tokens of my personal esteem will be worth five sons more to me than a draft for thirty-eight thousand dollars and some cents to cover your shipping charges. Fa Sien-seng, I give you thanks for honouring my humble house; Ho Sien-seng, I thank you and to you both safe journeys. The meagre draft is together with the unworthy porcelains."

The springless cart lurched suddenly forward as a gust blew from off the Gobi. So the blunt features and the bowing figure of Mr. Tsao were soon lost to view in a cloud of dust.

· · · · · ·

IV

MANCHURIANA

A<small>LTHOUGH</small> my ten years' sojourn in North China embraced no more than a twenty months' assignment in Manchuria, that period, during which my commercial activities were based on the then Japanese-controlled port of Dairen, remains, in retrospect, the most colourful phase of my career.

Rich in its diversity of Race and Custom, my District represented a broad field about which I roamed more or less at will. From time to time I furnished my Taipans with a Trade Report which, while couched in optimistic terms, was generously studded with the non-committal "If . . ." and I trusted it, probably more than they did, to serve as a sufficiency of token to justify my journeyings. I was enabled, less officially, to become an interested observer amid the increasing tempo of political developments in an environment so aptly described by my friend Owen Lattimore as "Cradle of Conflict".

Though my contemporary reflections are more generally recorded in the lighter vein, the entries in my diary on four consecutive days during the summer of 1928 no less bear witness to almost incredible contrasts in character and backcloth on a stage where now-shadowy players once made their moments of history.

On this particular Friday evening it appears that in company with a few fellow members of English, American, Danish and

German nationality, I lent casual ear to one, Yosuke Matsuoka, propounding some surprisingly pro-British views over the bar of the Dairen Club. In those days he was an official of the South Manchuria Railway, and I doubt if any among his cosmopolitan acquaintances of that period mistook Japan's subsequent Foreign Minister for a person possessed of much deep sincerity. Within a few years the world was to become witness to his worth.

The following afternoon found me some distance beyond the borders of the Kwantun Leased Territory dissipating my slender assets on the race course at Newchwang. Apart from the contrast between Japanese and Chinese-controlled territory, the significance of the occasion lies in little more than the entry of a name recording the fact that my company included that of a young English girl, who while exercising her pony on the same course a few months later, was kidnapped and held to ransom by Chinese bandits.* The subsequent story of her courage and resource in captivity did much more than merely hold the international headlines and stir public imagination for several weeks: her imperturbable bearing in the face of constant ordeals and threats restored much that had tended to dwindle in the way of British prestige in the impressionable minds of the Chinese. But in my journal for the day she, like the then equally unknown Matsuoka, figures as no more than a name: and the contrast has lost nothing of its significance in the passing of two decades. The one name creeps away into ignominious oblivion through a sinister chapter of dark history, whilst the other will always survive among the brighter legends of youthful courage.

* "Tinko" Pawley—the daughter of the Resident British doctor in Newchwang.

Turning the page, I find two lines recorded for the Sunday, sufficient in themselves to flood the mind with a torrent of oddly-assorted memories; many of them now diffuse and intangible: but a few there are that remain fresh and as clearly defined as though they might be no more than the happenings of a month ago. It appears that overnight I had travelled many miles further North and spent the day on the Mukden Golf course participating in a four ball with "The Young Marshal".

Chang Hsueh Liang was thus known, the better to distinguish him from his father—Chang T'so lin—who in turn was referred to as "The Old Marshal". Normally, Chinese War Lords are not among the characters whom one would have either the inclination or the opportunity to cultivate: but there was much that was exceptional in the personality of my golfing companion. I liked him because, in contrast to my foreign friends who took my unexpected descents upon them with somewhat weary forbearance, he, busier and overburdened by far greater responsibilities, always made a show of being genuinely delighted to see me.

"The Young Marshal" was, I believe on his own merits, a great soldier and an able administrator: but some of his shots to the green were inclined to be rather more than mildly erratic. I always imagined his golf had about it much the same limits of prowess as those manifest in his father's excursions into the game of Poker.

I have no first-hand evidence of what went on when "The Old Marshal" sat down at the table with half a dozen of his army commanders and the hands were dealt out: but I gleaned a fairly authoritative picture from one of his Generals who was shrewd enough in the first place to teach him the game. And his is a name that figures in my journal for the same day: what a wealth of reminiscence is conjured up through mention of "One Arm" Sutton,—quite the most colourful Englishman I ever met! In one respect he was comparable with the immortal Vicar of Bray; in that whatsoever War Lord was in power, Frank Sutton was still a General in the Chinese Army. Seemingly he could raise regiments from the Gobi dust and train them to a strange state of perfection: he found equipment, procured arms, negotiated anything or everything, dictated his own terms and invariably became indispensable to whoever could afford his services. At the end of each Poker session "The Old Marshal," who was invariably the big loser, handed round I.O.U's. for fabulous sums to the Generals sitting round him who politely accepted them in lieu of their winnings. If they valued their jobs, or more than likely their heads, none of them would ever have the temerity to present their bits of paper at a later date: that is, none of them except "One Arm" Sutton, whose tokens were immediately honoured without question. Then from time to time, this true Soldier of Fortune would purchase for half their face value the I.O.U's. handed to the other Generals which, at a strategic opportunity he would present as his own to "The Old Marshal," in return receiving full measure. In those years Frank Sutton certainly rode the high places of North China.

I reflect now how "The Old Marshal" was strategically liquidated through a railway "accident" of distinctly Japanese "design" and how, some years later, "The Young Marshal," with what I am convinced were motives more patriotic than personal, kidnapped his Generalissimo—Chiang Kai-shek,—

for which "indiscretion" he was subsequently shorn of his rank and offices and banished into ignominy. I believe he was such a man who might have changed the present unhappy history of China: be that as it may, I can only hope that off-stage he may have used the opportunity to improve his approach shots and that one day I may enjoy the privilege of introducing him to "The Far" at Hoylake. As for "One Arm" Sutton—well, it is anybody's guess: if he is alive his feet will not be resting on the mantelpiece, and if it should be unhappily otherwise, I am perfectly certain that they would be encased in his boots when it happened.*

I observe that on the fourth night I lent my no doubt willing patronage to a rendezvous which must be known to the majority of those who in their time have travelled the Trans-Siberian railway and countless others who have found occasion to tarry in that once-gay city where East and West indeed meet. I refer to "The Fantasia" in Harbin, where one danced with a Russian Countess for fifty cents in Mexican currency, or with the younger element among the Grand Duchesses who might well demand the inclusion of a bottle of bogus champagne into the bargain. Who shall say that those were not the days! But I shudder to think, in *these,* what has become of those Tsarist refugees from the Bolshevic terror, whose escape tales, invariably culminating in the final swim across the Sungari river into China, were always stirring and more than likely, in some cases, genuine too.

So much for the broad canvas: certainly in that cradle of conflict there was the spice of variety in a District Manager's life. But inevitably most of it had, perforce, to be spent

* I have recently learnt that unhappily he died in 1942 in a Japanese prison-camp in Hong Kong.

attending to generally mundane routine in the less colourful environment of Dairen. The office staff consisted of a dozen Chinese clerks all thoroughly loyal and impeccably honest, with the addition of one Japanese interpreter whose principal function was to translate the changing complications in the decrees of his fellow countrymen who unimaginatively administered the Kwantung Leased Territory and whose insatiable, child-like curiosity in our business affairs was inclined to impair one's patience.

My arrival in Dairen coincided with the necessity of recruiting on to the office strength a new such Japanese employee: preferably one guaranteed against emulating the performance of his two immediate predecessors in the position, who, each in turn, had absconded with considerably more than their lawful share of my Company's assets. Though as administrators, and *en masse* I never came to love the Japanese, it would be untrue and unjust not to admit that I developed quite a warm affection for several among them whom I met in Dairen. I was grateful to Mr. Kasheda on two counts: firstly because, from the moment of his arrival, his serio-comic approach to the appointment afforded me much quiet amusement: secondly, since it was a full three months after I had subsequently handed over to my successor and left for England on leave, that Mr. Kasheda decided to display his own remarkable exhibition of rascally craftsmanship and so, alas! followed his predecessors into the more restricted atmosphere of prison life. Any lesser sin he might have been forgiven, for "Kashie" was a character if ever one lived. On applying in person for the job, he announced himself to me in these terms. "I am very many different kinds of office clerk, also interpretations and type-writer."

He scored a bull with his first assignment which was to accompany me to the Japanese Administrative Offices and assist me in obtaining a licence to drive a motor cycle and sidecar. The practical test was easy until my Examiner, sitting in the side-car on a precipitous slope, ordered me, through the medium of Mr. Kasheda, who was clinging to me like a limpet from the pillion, to reverse the combination up hill. We passed that over when my Interpreter, explaining that the vehicle was not geared for such a manoeuvre, suggested that we all dismount and push. In the written test he apologised to the Examining Official for his failure to understand the technicalities involved in the paper, only to extract from his fellow countryman the confession that he, too, found himself in a similar quandary. This led to a great deal of head scratching and loud intakes of breath from the two of them, whilst I bent helplessly over a series of questions composed in what was to me the quite uncommunicative calligraphy of Japan. The hopeless situation was relieved by a sudden stroke of brilliant inspiration on the part of Mr. Kasheda. "Why not," he suggested in effect, "procure the list of answers, then I can inform the student what the questions mean." The suggestion was adopted and oddly enough it seemed that neither Examiner nor Interpreter appeared to sense any touch of irregularity about the manner in which the difficulties were so successfully overcome.

The incident may seem incredible but everyone who has lived in close association with the Japanese, apart from those who have suffered under them in prison camps, knows that they are a nation handicapped in their serious mindedness by an entire lack of any sense of the ridiculous, which largely explains why they are a race so rich in unconscious humour.

Mr. Hamamaura was a classic example of this. He was not only the (subsequently unfortunate) guarantor of Mr. Kasheda, through whom I came to meet him, but he also was the editor of a publication printed in English known as *The Manchuria Daily News*.

He disdained the friendliest approaches from myself and others, professing a slightly better knowledge of the English tongue, to edit his evening rag, free, gratis and for no more than the avoidance of its ridicule. Mr. Hamamaura would not have it. So it came about that the British residents of Dairen from time to time reaped a minor reward from the proprietors of *Punch* by the inclusion in that classic of what came to be known as M.D.N. Masterpieces. Among innumerable others, such as the stabilising of the Harbin dollar "by hooks or by crooks," came the announcement that a cocktail party had been held in the Dairen Club for the Captain and *Wardrobe* officers of H.M.S. *Ambrose*. *Punch's* comment, "We should like to see them dress ship," was apt: but far from dismaying Mr. Hamamaura he swept the political headlines into oblivion and announced in the boldest type at his disposal that "ONCE AGAIN WE FIGURE IN LONDON PUNCHES". Then, following an accurate account of the recognition, proceeded to deplore the fact that after so many of its extracts appearing in the London weekly, his own by now hardly less famous publication should continue to be referred to by *Punch* as "Manchuria paper" instead of it being afforded more specific recognition as *The Manchuria Daily News*.

If I had no more than a weakness for Mr. Kasheda and Mr.

Hamamaura, I had a genuine affection for Mr. Furasawa.
During my time he was captain of the Hoohigaura Golf Club
and many an unequal round we played together according to
our individual interpretation of the rules. Mr. Furasawa maintained that the ball might be teed up in close proximity to
the spot where it rested during its passage down the fairway.
Having been brought up in a somewhat more rigid school, I
thought differently: thus so long as we continued to enjoy each
other's company on the golf course, the Captain invariably
won by no less than eight and six. There was, however, the
sole and classic occasion on which I beat him. If I rightly
remember he lost his ball at each of the first four holes, was
out of bounds at the fifth and sixth, and drove into the rough
with only slightly better effect at the next eleven. At the
eighteenth he hit a cracking drive straight into the bunker
above the green. That was the last straw. The next evening I
played with an American visitor and discovered that the
Captain had exercised his privileges to the full: he had lost no
time in ordering large areas of rough to be hewn, the boundaries, where necessary, to be modified, and the bunker at the
eighteenth to be brought fifty yards nearer the tee.

At least Mr. Furasawa had a fair working knowledge of the
game, which was considerably more than that enjoyed by the
lesser lights among his fellow countrymen. I well remember
waiting for my partner on the first tee and witnessing an
exhibition by a pair of Nipponese novices at the game, which,
incidentally Mr. Kasheda always chose to term "The Imperial
and Ancients". They had equipped themselves in "plus-fours"
which, with a fine disregard for the knee fastenings, fell loosely
about their ankles. Between them they took a round dozen of

shots before finishing with the first tee, and at least a further two score more before arrival, with a misguided sense of direction, on the eighteenth green, handily situated fifty yards to starboard. It was then that they considered it appropriate to consult the book—an illustrated manual by Walter Hagen—and the sight has remained embedded in my mind of two incongruous and recumbent little men, pin high, opposite one another, solemnly studying the lie of their putts!

It perhaps seems odd how certain ineffectual incidents of this nature still claim memory's particular attention on a canvas so charged with an over-all impression of contemporary foreboding. But it was something typically Japanese that dubbed them for the stupid race they were. It may not be irrelevant to consider it in terms of to-day in our nearer sphere, when one's dark despair of any certainty for the future is suddenly illumined through the incidence of some utterly immaterial happening that is delightfully British and sufficient to restore full confidence in the character of one's kind.

I recall an incident which occurred along the Yamagata Dori in Dairen in 1928. The then-young Chichibu, brother of the Emperor, was due to drive along the wide thoroughfare, flanked by its modern buildings, at noon. An hour earlier the Japanese police had removed every resident along the route from the height of their normal precincts to the level of the street. Even the half-step high of the pavement was debarred from the public, since intricate calculation could not make it certain that its eminence might not afford the tallest among the populace the outrageous opportunity of looking down upon a passing Prince. Then, as he emerged from our office on a cold morning, Mr. Kasheda unexpectedly bumped into Mr. Tanaka who had simultaneously stepped out on the pavement from next door. I was subsequently to learn that the two of them had not met since an era of earlier struggle in the classroom of some secondary school situated in the far-away prefecture of Shimakosa. Simultaneous faint cries of mutual recognition were followed by almost inexhaustible intakes of breath as, oblivious to the world about them, each paid homage towards the other by assuming the attitude of a right angle, whilst poised slightly above the level of the multitude. The courtesies which demanded that the privilege of rising first be granted to him of greater accomplishment, naturally prolonged these pleasantries; polite enquiries on the subject of current status being, perforce, through their extravagant postures, addressed less audibly to one another than to the unaiding surface of the pavement. Mr. Kasheda was dressed in a foreign suit and, out of deference to visiting royalty, had left his overcoat at home. Mr. Tanaka was garbed with a greater degree of glamour: he wore wooden sandals and a flowered kimona, while about his neck was draped a seedy-looking fox with a startled expression, the whole being topped by a bowler hat.

This ludicrous scene was temporarily cut short by the descent of two police batons upon a pair of inviting posteriors, accompanied by a peremptory command that further deliberations must be carried on at a lower level. They obeyed the injunction in precise terms and after shuffling sideways from the pavement, still inclined in each other's direction, proceeded to settle the issue in the gutter.

If I have appeared to labour this incident, it is for the reason that at the moment of its happening, I seemed to sense one thing for certain. Thinking of the quick humour of the London

Cockney and the slow drollness of the Middle Westerner in relation to the scene before me, I knew instinctively that when war came, though we might suffer long at their hands, while God was in his Heaven, such a race would never get us down.

. . . .

V

THE ATTACHÉ CASE

HIDDEN away somewhere in The Attaché Case is the solution to a problem which has vexed me for twenty years. Time and again I have rummaged through it, never being quite certain if I found the right answer or not. So now I propose to relate the bare facts of the story concerning it, in order that others, no doubt cleverer than I, may decide for themselves whether the man I met, and met once more but never again, was simply sincere—or most supremely subtle. Here, then, it is.

. . . . . .

In the spring of 1929 I had been in China a full five years having served my Company, first in Tientsin, subsequently in the humidity of the Yangtse valley and for the past eighteen months as District Manager in the more invigorating climate of South Manchuria. I was due for relief and a spell of leave in England and on the eve of departure was paying a last round of calls on certain of our up-country Agents.

I sat in the lavishly-appointed observation car at the rear of the North-bound express which always pulled out of Dairen station punctually at 9.30 each morning and adhered to an immaculate time-table over the whole of its route. The

Japanese ran the South Manchuria Railway Company with its wide ramifications, hotels, hospitals, schools and half the industries of the Kwantung leased Territory, with clock-work precision. Everything was ordered exactly in accordance with the rules, and a grim air of determined efficiency brooded over each venture of this vast political organisation. The world knows now, as many of us then surmised would be the case, how the railroad, running like a wedge through nearly the whole length of Manchuria with its concessional mile of Japanese Territory on either side, was no mean factor in Nippon's later conquest of the three Eastern Provinces subsequently to be known as Manchukuo.

Sitting opposite me, rather upright in his easy chair, and dressed in the elegant blue gown of a less swashbuckling citizen was a Chinese war-lord. From time to time he marshalled into less straggling array, with the aid of a miniature comb, the thin drooping ends of a pair of conventional whiskers. With a fair sense of positioning, in a somewhat intricate territorial situation, his two thinly-disguised body-guards stood, seldom out of view, in the corridor adjoining our coach. Beside the war-lord, in contrast but also without his accoutrements, lounged a young Assistant Military Attaché from the American legation in Peking who had immediately made himself known to me.

The fourth occupant of the observation car, who completed our purely chance and oddly assorted party was no less a personage than the President of the Railway himself, literally monarch of all he surveyed, and in those significant years the biggest political factor outside Tokio. The President reclined a little distance away immersed in official documents but the persistent efforts of the young American to draw him into the conversation could not be long denied. With a somewhat deliberate air His Excellency stuffed his papers into a brief case and then proceeded to treat us to an account in faultless English of his youth and education abroad. He quoted both the classics and the scriptures and was obviously no mean historian. He provided us with a great deal of no doubt accurate information concerning the existing trend of Trade and Politics in nearly every country of consequence except, significantly enough, his own. To me, at least, he emerged on that occasion as a man of great charm and culture and, since I never saw nor indeed heard of him again, I like to retain the impression I formed of him that morning twenty years ago.

Our efforts with the War-lord were less productive. He indicated that he spoke no English and afforded us only mono-syllabic replies to remarks which the Attaché and I passed to him in Chinese. I was aware that he had received his military training in Japan and twenty-five years earlier had actively assisted in routing the Russians from the Kwantung Peninsula: but no words passed between him and the President. One presumed that relations between China and Japan in Manchuria were, even then, stretched beyond a point that would enable either of them to utilise the other's tongue without considerable loss of face. "The China Incident" was only a year or two away.

. . . .

The Attaché and I left the train at Mukden, but before doing so the American insisted on exchanging cards with the President and would have carried out the same courtesy with the War-lord had not the Old Marshal indicated with polite regret that he had not one readily available on his person.

I spent the remainder of the day with our Chinese Agent in Mukden who, speaking no English himself, was surprised and delighted that I should call upon him unaccompanied by an interpreter. It was a somewhat conceited experiment on my part, which I thought might improve my knowledge of Mandarin sufficiently to enable me to qualify for the Company's bonus before I went on leave. The Agent observed the elegancies sufficiently to show no signs of strain during the somewhat halting course of our deliberations and we parted on the most amicable terms of mutual admiration. But I had found the first leg of my experiment to prove a little exhausting and I was therefore relieved to have the somewhat easier, yet by no means more sincere, companionship of the American Attaché at dinner.

He became intensely interested when I told him that it was my intention to take the South Manchuria route on to Szeping-kai the following day, to spend the night there with my agent and then proceed by the less distinguished Chinese railway to Taonan, a city that stood on the borders of outer Mongolia and at the very edge of the Gobi desert. The Assistant Military Attaché was less concerned with Taonan than he was with the features of the railroad that was to lead me there. It was just a question of routine Intelligence and I told him that if he cared to dine with me in Dairen in a week's time, I felt I should be doing no one any disservice and saving him a lot of trouble by telling him then, the very simple facts he was seeking. He was thoughtful.

"Perhaps I should look it over myself."

"As you will," I replied. "But from what you tell me you've a lot of other ground to cover in a limited time and I can save you a couple of days at least. Of course, it's up to you."

We left it at that until the end of dinner when I was taking my leave of him, since I was due to make an early start on the morrow.

"It's been a pleasure to meet you," he remarked politely. "Will you take care of that little job for me? It would save me some valuable time." He fumbled in his notecase. "Here —take my card, and if I'm not in Dairen a week to-night, drop me a line before you leave.

I had the card in my hand as I went upstairs to my room, and as I put it down on my dressing table I was surprised to find that he had apparently handed me two by mistake. The first was inscribed in English and Chinese with his name and rank, quoting his address as the United States Legation (it had not then become an Embassy) in Peking. The second was printed in English and Japanese and bore the august name and status of His Excellency The President, who had handed it to my American friend that morning. I carefully preserved them both, hoping that I would remember to hand back the latter to the Attaché when next we met.

· · · · · ·

Some fifteen hours later I arrived at Szepingkai by the South Manchuria Railway, spent the late afternoon rapidly improving my Chinese conversation at our Agent's expense and put up for the night at a Japanese inn. By 7.30 the next morning I was back at Szepingkai station but on an isolated platform boarding

77

a train far less luxurious than those on which I had travelled during the past two days. It started an hour late with a lurch that threw me across the narrow compartment and then came to such an abrupt halt that I was immediately rocketed back into my seat again. This performance was repeated with sickening regularity throughout the long, slow journey towards Taonan. We stopped for seemingly interminable periods at an endless succession of wayside stations, with the sole object, apparently, of aiding the business of the local food vendors. We halted in between stations for no imaginable reason whatsoever. At one stopping place we entrained what seemed to amount to a complete Army Corps. They crowded out every inch of the compartments and corridors, massed themselves about the coach tops and clung like limpets to the running boards and even the buffers. They travelled with us for not more than ten miles and then spilled out in a seething grey mass on to a wayside platform, slowly sorting out themselves, their rifles and somewhat sparse equipment. I learnt that they had accompanied us as escorts through a notoriously infested bandit area and subsequently calculated that there must have been at least fifty troops for the protection of each individual passenger. In the early afternoon we spent a particularly long interlude at rest on what I noted to be one of the very few stretches of double track. This was in order to allow the daily South-bound train to pass on its way and as it went by I observed that it would have to take a chance with the bandits as the passengers were already overcrowding it, including the roofs, almost beyond the bounds of belief. As we jerked and jolted forward again I thought it was remarkable that we were a mere handful of passengers compared with what appeared to be a general exodus from the direction in which we were moving. What was happening in Taonan, I wondered. Was it civil war or famine or drought; any of these things can happen unexpectedly in the remoter parts of China without any means of forewarning to intending travellers. But the desire for sleep battled successfully with a curiosity which was more than mildly tinged with apprehension.

I awoke abruptly in the midst of a seething, shouting tumult of Chinese besieging the train on both sides. It was nightfall and I realised we must be drawing in to Taonan station. But what of the clamouring multitude, I thought. This is the end of the journey. Then it slowly dawned on me that the train returned South next morning and several thousand inhabitants of Taonan were desperately anxious to travel with it. I made to step out into the maelstrom that covered every inch of both platforms, but there was sheer panic abroad and the great mass surged forward and hemmed me in from each side. I resumed a bare six inches of what had been my seat and thought that in time the crowd might settle and enable me to emerge and go about my lawful occasions. But there was a babbling, excited, half-frightened score of men and women, children of all ages and very old people now jammed so tight around me that to move was an utter impossibility. Presently, above the sounds of commotion I heard the unmistakable tones of an Englishman talking in Chinese from the platform. He managed to squeeze his head in through the window.

"Room for an expectant mother?" he urged in the straight-forward manner of the native dialect. "Room for an expectant mother?"

"Thank heavens for that," I said in English, much to his

79

astonishment. "Here, let me out, just enough room for her here."

I had to employ the tactics of the Rugby scrum to force myself to the carriage door and on to the still crowded platform. But the way was kept clear for the young woman until she had gained my seat.

"That was a very noble gesture," said the Englishman. "But I think you'll be better on the roof anyway, if we can . . ."

"But look here," I explained. "I've been trying to get *out* of the train. I'm *arriving* you see, not departing."

"Arriving!" He stopped and looked at me. "What for? Are you a doctor?"

"No, I'm not, I'm . . ."

"Then you're a fool to come here at all. You must be crazy. Go on, hop up there and squeeze yourself amongst that mass on the roof—there's just room. You'll be there all night and probably fall off when the train starts to-morrow," he added cheerfully, "but it's safer than coming into the city."

"But what is it?" I asked. "Fire, or flood or . . ."

"Fire or flood! Good God man, don't you *know?* It's PLAGUE. They're dying like flies until we can get it under control. Now clamber up quick while you've still a chance."

I flung myself off the platform on to a buffer and began to hoist my body upwards.

"But what about you," I asked, as I noticed him threading his way back through the crowd.

"No: my job's in the city," he shouted back. "I'm a medical missionary."

. . . . . .

Through that long, chilly night and the longer journey back, I endured discomforts and alarms on the roof of that train which I can never recall to this day without something more than a shudder. I realised that we Westerners are far less inured to hardship and suffering than the great masses of Chinese, whose very existence hangs by such a slender thread. But I hung on feeling inordinately humble in the thought that they, like me, were running away, while an unknown Englishman stayed behind with cheerful courage to stem the tide of pestilence and death.

In the early afternoon of the following day we slid past the stationary North-bound train. From my precarious perch it was impossible to observe if it carried any passengers but by that time I was beyond caring and only desired most earnestly to return as speedily as possible to the sanctuary and solid comforts of Dairen. But when the train eventually pulled into Szepingkai I immediately realised that unless I could achieve something drastic, my escape from seething infection to personal security would still be considerably delayed. As I, and over a thousand of my fellow passengers, poured off every conceivable portion of the train we were hemmed in by a strong cordon of Japanese police all of whom wore protective masks over the lower part of their faces. We were then herded into a roped-in enclosure some distance away where there were already a considerable number of the previous day's travellers still awaiting medical examination by the Japanese authorities before being permitted within the territorial precincts of the South Manchuria Railway. It was a natural and quite reasonable precaution, but in my frustrated state of mind I regarded the whole affair as an outrageous assault on such dignity as was left to me.

The prospect of spending a further night and probably several hours of the next day exposed both to the elements and possible infection from so many inhabitants of plague-infested Taonan closely packed around me, was more than I was prepared to face. I sought out a policeman who in turn passed me on to someone in higher authority. Eventually I was escorted into a wooden hut where two Japanese doctors were engaged in scrutinising in turn a long, patient line of the previous day's passengers. I was regarded impassively but with certain signs of impatience. One of the doctors lowered his protective mask.

'You come," he asked, "from where?"

"I haven't *been* in the City of Taonan," I shouted impatiently. "I stayed in the train. I never went into Taonan: I . . ."

"Ah Taonan." He made that noise peculiar to the Japanese that is an audible drawing in of a deep breath through clenched teeth. "You must wait—have medical examinations."

I was about to remonstrate further when a more cultured, but no kinder-looking, official approached me.

"I am Doctor Tsuda of the South Manchuria Railway," he said politely. "If you have come in the train from Taonan you must wait your turn for medical examinations. I am very sorry."

I was vexed and overwrought.

"I shall complain bitterly about this," I protested, "unless you make an exception of me or examine me immediately."

He regarded me closely for a moment, then a sudden thought seemed to strike him. "You are an American?" he asked.

"I . . ." My tired mind was just able to focus on the possible significance of his question before committing myself either way, when he spoke again.

"You are Assistant American Military Attaché? I have notifications about him. If you have your card, please."

I was past endeavouring to account for this amazing turn of events. How did he know about my friend? Who had notified him? Perhaps the Attaché had heard what was going on in Taonan and had done some quiet work for me in the background, knowing that the card which he had given me would extend diplomatic privileges which my own could not achieve. I satisfied my conscience by presuming that the young American was working on the basis of one good turn deserving another, and sorting his card out from that of the President, which he had erroneously given me at the same time, I passed it over without further comment to Dr. Tsudo. He glanced at it, inhaled loudly through his teeth, inclined his body gracefully from the waist and said, "Very sorry. Please."

He led me out of a door behind the examining doctors, called two policemen and gave them certain instructions. I was still mildly apprehensive until I fully realised that they were escorting me back to Szepingkai station and on to the platform from which the South Manchuria Railway express was due to leave for Dairen in a few minutes. They stood rigidly by while I boarded the train and only after it started pulling effortlessly out did they incline themselves slightly forward, salute, then turn on their heels like a pair of automata.

I fingered the card in my pocket that bore the name of the President of this gigantic and coldly efficient organisation, then examined it closely before tucking it safely away in my notecase. What a story I should have to relate to my Attaché friend when I restored that card back to him in Dairen within the next few days and how grateful I felt to him for what I fondly imagined to be the subtle arrangements he had made on my behalf so as to prevent my being delayed a further twenty-four hours.

.   .   .   .   .   .

On the evening prior to the date of my departure from Dairen I gave a small dinner party at the Yamato Hotel. It was arranged in order to say "Farewell" to my particular friends amongst the British and American community and introduce them to my successor and his wife. It was a friendly, cheerful gathering, about a dozen all told. That, added to the prospect of a lazy, carefree five weeks at sea ahead of me in a new P. & O. liner, with England after a five-year absence at the end of the voyage, served to dispel from my mind the nightmare of my recent trip to Taonan. My one regret was that the young American Military Attaché had not shown up at the Dairen Club the previous evening in accordance with the arrangement we had made a week earlier in Mukden. I presumed that his travels must have delayed him and it was my intention at all costs to make a point of dropping him a line before I went to bed, enclosing the brief report I had prepared for him on the subject of the Taonan Railway and, of course, to restore to him the card of His Excellency the President.

Towards the end of dinner, my successor's wife, a bride recently arrived from home, drew my attention to the Japanese orchestra up in the balcony, who were playing "Rose Marie" even less tunefully than usual, and enquired why they carried on their activities behind a protective barricade of wire netting. I related how, when I first came to Dairen, I had asked the Hotel Manager the same question, and, regarding me impassively, he had supplied me with a straightforward answer. "Englishmens sometime make silly asses of Violin."

"The Japs—which, incidentally, you mustn't call them," I explained to her,—"are a severely practical breed of little men, essentially efficient, but possessed of about as much sense of humour as a coffin lid."

"You said it!"

I turned round quickly, for it was the unmistakable voice of the Attaché who was standing behind me.

"You said it!" he repeated, with a strange half-quizzical look on his boyish face.

"This is an unexpected pleasure for all of us," I said, as I greeted him and suggested he should join the party. "You're only about twenty-seven hours late."

He opened his mouth to speak, but it appeared that he was quite lost for words, and I immediately started introducing him all round. He repeated, as the best bred Americans invariably will, each name in turn so as to implant them upon his memory, and then proceeded, with a charm which matched his looks, to make himself thoroughly agreeable to everybody. I was aware that he cast occasional glances in my direction in the manner of such a man who has a tale to unfold as opportunity might offer, but in the meantime he would allow nothing to mar the spirit of the party. After a time he unexpectedly rose and proposed my health.

"To those who travel," he announced briefly, raising his glass and fixing me with a somewhat satirical look. My friends joined him with gay acclamation and then I rose, and, looking straight towards the Attaché I uttered the counter toast—"To those who don't."

His face wore a sardonic smile for several moments, then someone next to him claimed his attention. There was something in his expression that caused a sudden doubt to spring into my mind. With a certain apprehension I began to wonder. Later on I had a brief opportunity of a word with him across the table. I took out my notecase and amonst a mass of sailing tickets, emigration passes, medical certificates and the like, started searching for the President's card.

"There's something here I have to give you. You remember at Mukden you . . ."

"If you're talking about what I asked you to do for me in Mukden," he broke in, "forget it."

"Well—it's not quite that . . ." I started, but he had turned to the lady who sat on his left, so I put my case back in my pocket and continued my discourse on the idiosyncrasies of the Oriental to the bride from England.

When the ladies left us, the oldest and most respected British resident of Dairen turned to the man I had met on my recent travels.

"Tell me," he asked, "just what does an Assistant Military Attaché have to do?"

The American removed the cigar from his mouth.

"If that Assistant Military Attaché is me," he said, "he just has to do some damfool things."

We waited expectantly while he took another draw at his cigar.

"I met an English guy once—a generous kind of fellow," he recounted, avoiding my eye, "who offered to do a little job for me looking over a railroad in the North—maybe he did it, and maybe he had more sense if he knew better than I just

86

what was cooking in the North. I was still in the dark when I figured later on that I'd better go up and give that railroad the once-over myself. Boy, did I find plenty of trouble there. Thirty-six hours I spent at that railroad terminus and then came back on the coal tender of a locomotive. I'm not telling you why—maybe it might scare you. That was trouble enough, but when I got back among the Japs there was plenty more."

My throat felt suddenly parched and I finished my glass of whiskey in a single gulp.

"You see," went on the Attaché, "there was a reason why they had to hold on to everyone who'd travelled that route, for a while anyway, and I figured there would be close on five thousand of us milling about in a short time—four thousand, nine hundred and ninety-nine Chinese, lousy, if no worse, and me, just a stranger."

"But," broke in the oldest British resident, "as a member of the Legation surely you would only have to identify yourself —your card or something?"

" That's what I thought," went on the Attaché. "So I gave them a card and I yelled, ' Let me out of here quick'."

"Then what happened?" asked my successor.

"What happened! Well I'll tell you what happened: it was dark and they took it away and went into a huddle over it under a lamp. Then they came back and said, 'You try make one big fool of Japanese policemens,' and for that they kept me corralled with that mob of soiled celestials for two days and a night."

"But didn't you make a protest?" someone asked. "It's out-rageous."

"That's what I thought, especially since the American Consul discovered what was cooking after I'd left and officially requested that when I got back I should certainly not be detained."

"You told the Consul about it, of course," said the oldest British resident.

"No, *sir*," replied the Attaché.

"No?"

The American chuckled to himself for a few moments, then, "That's the pay-off," he said. "Just too late I realised that they were sore at me for trying to pass myself off as—who do you think?—His Excellency the President of the South Manchuria Railway."

"As *who?*" asked everyone except me.

"It was the only way I could figure it," he explained. "I had the old Nip's card among my own: he gave it to me when I met him a day or two earlier. I *must* have handed it out to them in the dark since it was missing when I looked for it next morning. They had a perfect right to get mad at me for trying to pass myself off as the railroad President. It was sure 'making one big fool of Japanese policemens'."

He turned to his original questioner. "So now, sir, you see the damfool things an Assistant Military Attaché has to do."

There was a clearing of throats and a general murmur of comment all round. After a slight pause I remarked, "What an intensely interesting story!"

"Yes," he said, as he rose and strolled with a casual air round to the back of my chair whilst the others discussed and debated his tale among themselves. Leaning forward, as though to convey a confidence to me, with his mouth cupped between his hands so that no one should overhear, he blew into my ear a rich, prolonged and most fruity "raspberry".

Then, with the friendliest smile and the warmest handshake he took swift leave of me, bowed to the others and was immediately gone.

. . . . . .

VI

JOURNEY WITH JASON HO

I SELDOM undertook any of my periodical trips into the interior of North China in the late 'twenties unless I could be accompanied by Jason Ho. He was never-failing as guide, philosopher and friend, and typical of so many millions of his fellow countrymen whose qualities are as rich in virtue as they are in complexity.

The correct English interpretation of his name was Ho Chai-sun: but Mr. Ho had, during some period of his remote youth, supplemented his still vague knowledge of the English language with readings from the Odyssey and had been much impressed by the story of the Golden Fleece. It required only the slightest phonetic change to merge his supplementary name of Chai-sun into the style of Jason and so it was as Jason Ho that he signed himself.

There is no accounting for it, but it is an accepted fact that the great majority of Chinese employed by foreign business concerns in North China emanate not from Ningpo, but from some suburb of that port which they invariably describe as "Ningpo-more-far". Jason Ho was no exception in this respect and indeed took pride in the fact that he, too, was a native of "Ningpo-more-far". Apart from that, he was almost strangely uncommunicative about himself. His nature as well as his features were essentially impassive. He might, for instance, have been any age between the early thirties and the late fifties and since it is not entirely in accordance with the elegancies of Chinese etiquette to enquire into such matters, I never satisfied my curiosity in that respect.

The most hazardous journey we took together was in the summer of 1928 when we travelled two hundred miles up the Yalu river to Linkiang. Our object was to break new ground in exploring the possibilities of extending British trade and appointing, on my firm's behalf, a Chinese agent in a somewhat inaccessible region of Manchuria. I was particularly thrilled at the prospect of this trip since to the best of my knowledge no Englishman had previously made the journey. Subsequent events proved this not to be surprising and it was entirely due to the calm ingenuity of Jason Ho that the expedition did not terminate in painful calamity.

The course of the Yalu forms the boundary between China and Korea. The River is about two miles wide where it flows into the Yellow Sea near the Chinese port of Antung but in its middle and upper reaches it narrows down to never more than half a mile in width as it progresses precariously by gorges and rapids with the high mountains of Manchuria on the one side and the gentler slopes of Korea on the other.

Some of the scenery is indescribably beautiful and compensated for the rigours and discomforts of a several-day journey. Whilst by day there seemed a certain magic in the vast spaciousness of these surroundings, it invariably left one at night with an inescapable consciousness of one's own insignificance. It was a sensation that became more intensified as we journeyed by slow stages further into the unknown interior.

But to return to the beginning of our journey. Jason Ho and

I were ferried across the river from Antung to Korea accompanied by a packing case full of tinned foods, a quantity of bedding which enfolded a change of clothes, a first-aid outfit, a camera, a portable typewriter, and—I never learnt where Jason Ho found it—a crate of bottled lager.

Immediately we set foot on their territory, in those days very much under Japanese domination, the authorities regarded us with the gravest suspicion and immediately took possession of the camera. The customs officials obviously believed in doing their job thoroughly. They took most of my portable typewriter to pieces, displaying a child-like interest in its construction and Mr. Ho's subsequent efforts to reassemble it occupied him at various intervals for six days. Their next outrage was to remove every cigarette from my case and rubber stamp each one of them individually with a large purple hieroglyphic. They confiscated the first-aid outfit but heeded little over the provisions, the bedding and the beer. We eventually presumed that they were well aware, as we subsequently learnt, that we should have to travel without them and it is probably superfluous to remark that we never saw any trace of these various possessions again.

It seemed appropriate that the only English those Japanese officials appeared to know were the four words "Very sorry for you" which they repeated at frequent intervals. We had already begun to feel very sorry for ourselves, a state of mind which was in no way alleviated by the discovery of the craft that was to convey us to some remote part of Korea from where we hoped to cross over to China again in search of Linkiang.

The boat was a somewhat elongated variety of sampan about

thirty feet in length and maybe a third of that in width. It boasted a covered waggon effect over what was destined to serve as passenger accommodation while in the stern sheet was a petrol engine designed to rotate a three-bladed aeroplane propeller. The shallows and rapids of the Yalu naturally precluded employment of the more ordinary forms of marine propulsion or indeed the use of other than essentially flat-bottomed craft. The cargo-carrying native boats normally complete the journey between Antung and Linkiang in about six weeks. We hoped to be there by means of this hydroplane affair in as many days.

It is no exaggeration to say that the accommodation might have been sufficient to house four persons, in cramped surroundings, but without undue discomfort, for a period not exceeding half an hour. It was therefore somewhat disconcerting to discover that the "passenger list" included a mixture of some forty Chinese, Koreans, and Japanese of both sexes and all ages with a week's journey ahead of us. Eventually we were all battened down with the canvas top reaching to a height of four feet above the ship's bottom and it needed only the roar of the aeroplane propeller above us to complete my worst conception of purgatory.

My fellow passengers, apart from Jason Ho and one or two others, appeared a nondescript lot. Demanding attention, however, was an immense Korean whom I sized up as a well-to-do merchant. In some respects he was perhaps more fortunate than the many, for as he squatted on his allotted few inches of ship's space he housed within the crook of either arm as pretty a pair of Geisha girls as I had yet set eyes upon. Obviously more comfortable than any, however, was a Colonel of the Imperial

Japanese army with definite ideas of *Lebensraum*. He sat at ease, as it were, and by spreading out his heavily spurred extremities as far as they would reach, ensured for himself four times his normal share of accommodation. Obviously a selfish and conceited man, his eventual departure from our midst some two days later was in a manner most pleasing to his fellow travellers.

His command, consisting of a battalion of infantry, complete with band, were drawn up waiting for him on some otherwise obscure stretch of the Korean bank. The craft drew in as near as possible to the river's edge and a gang plank was thrown ashore. Directly the Colonel's head appeared from under the "covered waggon" the battalion presented arms and the band struck up what I presumed to be the Japanese equivalent of the General Salute. The Colonel took one step forward on to the gang plank but that was as far as he reached before one of those spurs that had caused us no little discomfort became attached to an idle boathook and he was immediately catapulted into three feet of intervening water. It was an inspiring spectacle from every point of view for not a muscle moved among his rigid troops ashore, nor was there even the suggestion of a gurgle in the heavier brasses of the band that was doing him honour. After the splash had subsided the Colonel was observed dripping with slime and up to the waist in water fishing for his cap. When he had retrieved this and emptied from it a pint of Yalu river he solemnly replaced it on his head and proceeded to return the salute of his command. I was undecided whether the incident was indicative of iron discipline or just an example of the natural reactions of a humourless, unimaginative breed. I did not know. But I do know that the swashbuckling little fellow, probably smelling to high heaven, had scrambled up the river bank and the craft had pushed off into the stream again before Jason Ho and I and the others dared laugh.

I think if the rest of us had known that such a scene was to be enacted for us we might better have endured the agonies and discomforts, particularly of the first two days. It was when the first eating time came round in that foetid overcrowded atmosphere that I found it expedient to start bribing the Korean mechanic to let me share his stand by the engine and the roaring propellor. He was quite adamant in his refusals until for the third time on the first day's journey the engine broke down and we had eventually drifted back almost to our starting point. I knew then even less than I know now concerning the mysteries of the internal combustion engine, but I can relate with every confidence that my knowledge was more advanced than that of the Korean mechanic. When I had successfully got things moving in the right direction on two occasions and had given away most of my gaily embossed cigarettes, I finally achieved at least temporary escape from that virtual hell-hole of a covered waggon.

We always found respite, however, during the hours of darkness for the craft tied up alongside the nearest Korean village and the passengers slept at the local inn. True to Japanese influence, even the meanest Korean hostelry was equipped with its bath house but my only fellow travellers who shared with me the advantage of these amenities were the Korean merchant and his two Geisha. I was always mildly embarrassed when the Innkeeper's wife or daughters took it as a matter of course that they should assist me in my ablutions: but whilst I always succeeded in maintaining my independence in this respect I could of course raise no objection to the presence of the tired business man in the bath alongside me, nor to the fact that after having had his back scrubbed by his two girl friends he invariably returned the compliment by subsequently affording them similar assistance with no merely assumed air of complete indifference. I learnt that this was no more than a freely recognised courtesy amongst the Koreans and Japanese who regard the bath house as a social meeting ground for both sexes. I also came to the conclusion that here existed one of the many fundamental differences in outlook between the Japanese and the Chinese; for Jason Ho was both shocked and horrified by the communal nature of these proceedings and intimated that such "goings on" would never be countenanced in the " .Washbody shop" he occasionally frequented in "Ningpo-more-far".

There were no doubt Chinese inns on the Manchurian side of the river as well, but apart from never calling there it was noticeable that the craft maintained a course as close to the Korean bank as possible over the entire journey. It was only too well known that the Chinese riverside villages were the happy hunting-ground of bandit hordes who made a substantial living through plundering the merchandise that was traded up the Yalu and, as opportunity afforded, held up any well-to-do travellers to ransom. I was never indifferent to an awareness that a Foreigner, or a "Big-nose" as they call us, employed by one of the principal commercial concerns was a prize which might come their way but once in a lifetime. Several British and American travellers had indeed been taken captive in the less accessible regions of Manchuria during recent months and their release had subsequently been negotiated by their employers for, in most instances, very considerable sums of money. If such a fate befell me I imagined my chief apprehension would be the possibility of my Directors considering that in view of the price demanded in return for my release being entirely out of proportion to my value it would be more in the interest of the shareholders to let me rot. It was food for thought.

On the sixth day we finally disembarked, with no feeling of regret, from our still overcrowded craft and sought out a ferry to take us across the river to Linkiang. But first of all there were preparations. Jason Ho insisted that I should clothe my person in the blue garb of a Chinese peasant. He intimated that by this means I should direct less attention to myself by appearing, as he put it, "less extraordinary". I am glad he did not suggest that I should find the means whereby I might contract an attack of jaundice as well, in order to complete the illusion we were seeking. I supposed we had to take a chance on the colour of my skin and the shape of my eyes.

At all events in such manner did we arrive in the Chinese town that was apparently hitherto unknown to the Westerner. There was nothing to distinguish it from a score of native cities I had previously visited in the interior and we steadfastly explored the possibilities of trade and after several days completed the somewhat prolonged negotiation in the appointment of a certain Mr. Wong to be our Agent.

It was altogether rather a tricky business, considerably complicated by the fact that Jason Ho felt it expedient to explain at great length to Mr. Wong that I was not the accredited representative of my Company at all. I was introduced into the picture as being merely a quite impecunious missionary from Antung who was acting as go-between in negotiating an arrangement which would prove of mutual benefit to both parties. My commission and only reward in accordance with

Chinese custom in such cases would be five dollars from each side. Jason Ho, in his usual flowery style, told our prospective agent this fabulous story in such a convincing manner that it seemed indeed Mr. Wong actually believed it. At any rate when the negotiations were complete and the "chops" applied to a document already prepared by Mr. Ho, I was handed my five dollars commission with due ceremony. It subsequently took many months to credit the sum back to our agent through the accounts bit by bit in such a way that it might escape his attention.

We could have saved ourselves the trouble for a year later Mr. Wong decided to discover the world that lay beyond a small stretch of the Yalu river and unexpectedly returned my call in the Company's spacious premises in Dairen. There he caught the impecunious missionary from Antung sitting among the polished spittoons and other refinements of a District Manager's office. Whether it was to save his own face or mine, or possibly both, he blandly expressed his appreciation of having eventually received the last instalment of the five dollars and added that of course our subterfuge had not for one moment deceived him, but he was nevertheless generous in expressing his obvious admiration for such cunning that had served no small purpose in baffling the wits of Mr. Fu.

Mr. Fu, accompanied by two less prosperous-looking characters had paid us a visit the night before we went down river again from Linkiang. He was a gentleman possessed of great courtesy but extreme curiosity. The discussion which we had together was carried on in an atmosphere of extreme politeness with a full measure of tea drinking and the age-old elegancies that are essentially Chinese. But if Mr. Fu was suave he had nothing of the persuasion of Jason Ho. In answer to certain rather urgent questions which were put to him concerning me, Jason, at great length, related that although I was indeed a missionary I had through some miscarriage of justice recently been unfrocked and disowned by my particular Society. He declared with the utmost conviction that I was now a person quite devoid of background or associations and no longer of the slightest interest to my relatives or friends. In fact he contrived, with complete success, to present me as the world's biggest bum, and dressed up as I was like a Chinese coolie with two weeks' uneven growth about my features, I was quite certain I must have looked it.

It was as well, for though his appearance and manner might suggest otherwise, we were left in no doubt whatsoever that in a country where there is refinement as well as honour among thienes, Mr. Fu was a bandit of more than local renown.

Nothing perturbed Mr. Ho. I have often reflected how only his ingenuity and powers of invention were responsible for saving me the indignity of having one of my ears placed on the Board Room table with a demand for a hundred thousand dollars before further portions of my anatomy were delivered for the contemplation of my Directors.

Jason Ho was, and I hope and pray still is, a unique, impassive personality, asking little of a slender life that at its best was but meagre. Yet I never felt richer than when in his company, nor prouder than by the privilege of his friendship and—I have always hoped—his affection.

· · · · · ·

VII

AH FAT

B ORNE, a light burden, on wings from ten thousand miles
away, there came back for me the other day the echo of
an era that ended fifteen years ago.

It was a letter from Ah Fat.

There was little enough in it that mattered: nothing at any
rate to compare with the knowledge that my old Chinese
House-boy still survived, and the gratification it afforded me
to be remembered particularly as "Deer Masta", from which I
sensed that, in his changing world, he, at least, had not absorbed
new ideologies.

But then, of course, Ah Fat never absorbed anything. From
the evening in 1927, when I came home and found that he had
taken possession of my bungalow at Hoshigaura until I bade
farewell to him on the Shanghai Bund in 1934, he steadfastly
remained the jealous guardian of an unalterable law that was
utterly his own. He was quite impassive, philosophical even in
the face of nigh-catastrophic emergency, resourceful beyond
the degree of genius, and capable of experiencing no insult save
one, the outrage of inference that his rather tawdry time-piece
was somewhat out of true. Only once, save when I was on the
point of departure, did I suggest that his cherished watch was
wrong, and never again considered such comment good token
for the several unaccountable little "accidents" that followed.

His letter, arriving in austerity England where there are but few survivals among those who more than disdainfully "oblige", served to recapture what was for me an atmosphere of essentially spacious days, glancing back on which I find that my reflection may well afford a smile.

.   .   .   .   .   .

I had brought my own boy to Dairen when I was transferred to Manchuria from Hankow in 1927; but he was never happy, being obviously ill at ease in the leased territory under Japanese jurisdiction, and homesick for his native province of Hunan and the sultry clime of the Yangstze valley. So I wired my predecessor, and he in turn despatched an urgent missive to his former retainer, who had retired from service to eke out a sufficiency of well-won wage and supplementary "squeeze" in that elastic and indefinable district known as Ningpo-more-far. That was all I knew, until the evening on which I returned from Dairen to my bungalow at Hoshigaura seven miles away, accompanied by two friends, and found the then quite unfamiliar features of Ah Fat, expanding over an immaculate white gown from the nether end of which protruded a pair of neatly-bound trouser bottoms over the conventional carpet slippers. He was assuming an attitude on the door step that was at once expectant and imperial.

"Where's Fong?" I asked, referring to my boy from Hankow.

"Have go, Masta," came the immediate reply. "Coolie have go too. To-morrow me find new coolie."

"But . . ."

101

"Me have pay month's wages. Me fix all ploper fashion. Me b'long Ah Fat. Me ..."

"So you're Ah Fat! Before you work for Mr. ..."

"Yes, Masta. Masta, me have fix chow—three men. Just now me take cock-a-tail, shake plenty much, from ice-box."

My friends and I relaxed on the verandah and presently found ourselves imbibing the most delectable Martinis, accompanied by a wide variety of "small eats". Both of them were birds of passage, having travelled from Europe on the Trans-Siberian Railway and unexpectedly walked into my office less than two hours earlier; but it seemed that Ah Fat not only knew they would arrive with me at the bungalow, but moreover appeared to be fully conversant with all our particular tastes. As he waited on us at table, with an air of quiet and utterly unobtrusive efficiency, Maynard's glass was filled and replenished with whiskey, Harcourt's with orange squash, and mine with a special brand of lager beer. There was no questioning as to which or any of us took our coffee black or otherwise; it was all exactly right and at ten, precisely, there was a motor car at the door to drive us to a Russian cabaret called "The Babylon", where a table had been booked so that we might indulge our fancies for an hour before my friends caught their boat to Shanghai. It is no use endeavouring to fathom how such a knowledge of one's habits or inclinations gets abroad in China; it just remains one of those unsolved mysteries of the East into which it is frequently, perhaps, not as well to enquire.

During my spell in Manchuria and later, Ah Fat was ever immaculate, always there with limitless meals at all hours, a sufficiency of drinks to suit all tastes and on no occasion was he either obtrusive or, indeed, even mildly apparent. He had what might be termed his idiosyncrasies, but few of them were out of common with the recognised procedure and the perquisites of his calling, the order of which he had, during his many years of experience in service to the Englishman, perfected to a fine art. We had the usual understanding, for instance, about the bill for soup-meat, which was invariably paid without creating loss of face through any insistence concerning its inspection: the soup-meat was just something which never materialised, except, possibly, in the strange shape of some native delicacy which Ah Fat and his assistant found particularly succulent. Then there was the ten per cent. discount for cash monthly on the Comprador's account, which that rascally vendor of foreign provisions apparently never honoured in accordance with his published terms. One refrained from asking about that either, since one was well aware that its allotment had also become an established precedent of menial perquisite. It was apt, however, to be mildly irritating if one invited the native tailor, the shirt-cutter or the shoe-maker to call in in his professional capacity on one's own premises; should he feel disinclined to pay the toll for admittance, or the recognised amount of levy on sub-sequent delivery of the finished article. If questions were asked, Ah Fat was ever ready with a wide variety of valid reasons as to why, for my own protection and the preservation of my face, I should honour a rival establishment with my patronage.

One bitter wintry afternoon, such as I have experienced no-where but in Manchuria, Ah Fat rang me up at the office and suggested I should secure a room at the Yamato Hotel for the night as the central heating at the bungalow had "broke up". The cost of my dinner and room was the price I had to pay for an insistence that a trial consignment of Japanese anthracite which I had ordered would be better suited to the furnace than the cheaper type of Chinese fuel organised by Ah Fat. I had, as it were, invited the imposition: but the affair of the "rain-water" seeping into the petrol tank of my motor cycle was a penance in no way deserved.

High-spirited as I was, it would have been unjust of Ah Fat to imagine that I deliberately contrived to detach from its moorings the sidecar in which he sat dozing over his shopping baskets while our high-powered combination was bowling round a slight curve in the highway at considerable speed. The nodding Ah Fat had proceeded on his solo expedition with only gradual loss in momentum for some distance along the road before the unleashed connecting rod hit the surface with a metallic screech, spun the sidecar round in a series of revolutions as remarkable as the pirouettes of an ice ballerina, then shot it up a bank where it turned turtle and came to rest in the middle of some trolley lines. Ah Fat was wide awake by the time I rejoined him and only slightly shaken. In one of his baskets had been two dozen eggs and a flimsy bag of flour. As I helped him to his feet he presented such an awe-inspiring spectacle that I was quite unable to restrain a rich and rude guffaw. Maybe it was that laugh that subsequently let the waters of heaven mingle with the spirits in my tank.

I think my old retainer was really at his best when he rejoined me in Tientsin after I had been on leave in England and subsequently when he came with me to Shanghai. The wider variety of social life in the larger ports allowed a greater degree of scope for his talents.

In actual fact when I left Dairen I had said good-bye to him, given him a generous *cumsha* and imagined that he would then disappear for ever within the fastness of his sanctuary at Ningpo-more-far. But I had a five-year further blessing. Returning to China from England at the end of 1929 I was booked to travel P. & O., but at the last minute decided to cancel my passage, travel to New York and from there to Los Angeles, where I stayed several days with friends, before catching a cargo boat across the Pacific. I made no advance bookings, gambling more or less on good fortune enabling me to report back at my Head Office in Shanghai on or about the date my leave expired. They were surprised to find in actual fact that I had returned a week early, fully expecting me to be on the P. & O. which had hardly yet arrived in Hong Kong. But Ah Fat was on the landing stage to greet me and impart the information that within two days "we" were being posted to Tientsin. It didn't surprise me: long since had I given up any idea of probing into Ah Fat's particular model of "bush radio". He seemed to know things which I didn't even know myself, nor to the best of my knowledge any one else was aware of either. Sufficient to relate that I was delighted at the re union and with the certainty in mind that henceforth all arrangements for my personal comfort and the things which I had been obliged to take thought of myself in England and America would now be adequately catered for. My life would resume its well-organised supervision—all ploper fashion!

In Tientsin I shared a mess with three other somewhat carefree young men: one was an American employed in oil, while the other two belonged to British concerns. In common with the great majority of foreigners working with prominent business interests in those days we all lived like fighting cocks, joined all the Clubs, ran cars, kept ponies, favoured the gay life, and now and then paid a few bills. We also each had our individual boys; but by mutual and simultaneous agreement on both sides, as it were, of the green baize door, Ah Fat became the undisputed major domo and answerable to us all for the manifold sins and omissions of the others. We learnt to respect his astuteness the hard way, particularly, for instance, in the matter of the rapidly-disappearing sherry which was a lesson in itself to us all.

"Matt", the American, was the one responsible for saying he'd "stop those so-and-so's from helping themselves to the Bristol Milk", and taking the half empty bottle, he poured us out one each, then filled it up again to its previous level, with a carefully-prepared liquid he had brought with him from the office, replaced the cork firmly and let matters rest for three days.

"I hope it isn't poison," somebody had said at the time.

"It won't quite kill 'em," was the reply, "but it'll give 'em a darned uncomfortable twenty-four hours."

I was then suddenly called up to Peking, and when I returned to the Mess two days later, was surprised to find all my three companions apparently suffering from what was known colloquially as "Tientsin Tummy". Instinctively I looked in the cupboard for the sherry bottle, found that its contents had shrunk to the level of the dregs and summoned Ah Fat. I had never seen him look so well, nor for a man of his years more sprightly which prompted me to enquire into the immediate health of the other servants, only to learn that they were all equally robust and hearty.

"Only other Mastas little bit ill," he said with a faint expression of concern.

"Ah Fat," I enquired, "which man drink sherry last two days?"

"Dlink shelley," exclaimed Ah Fat. "No man dlink shelley three days more: dlink gin."

I waved the well-nigh empty bottle at him. "How come then no man drink sherry, this before-time half full, now finish?"

Ah Fat's features bore no trace of emotion as he blandly replied, "Soup meat not easy Masta—every night must put lit' shelley in Mastas' soup. Suppose not put shelley . . ."

"That's alright, Ah Fat," I concluded hurriedly, "Go topside, take other three master hot rice pudding, then bring me whiskey soda—big fashion."

"Lice pudding," beamed Ah Fat, and shimmered out.

It was our practice to invite some of the junior officers from the British and American garrisons stationed in Tientsin, as well as a number of the younger foreign business element, to dine in our Mess about once a month. It never seemed to perturb Ah Fat, and his satellites if we asked half a dozen guests and, as frequently happened, about fifteen turned up. The food and drink was invariably adequate, since well-trained Chinese Houseboys are always prepared for such emergencies. And Ah Fat, in common with others of his calibre, had evolved a simple expedient for overcoming a sudden and embarrassing shortage in plates and cutlery: he took note of those present, and delayed dinner until he had communicated with their respective establishments and made arrangements for the guests' own utensils to be sent over. There was, of course, the unforgettable evening when a newly-arrived and rather stuffy British Major mistook our address for that of a very distinguished resident and drifted into the household just as one of our more hilarious and overcrowded parties was getting under way. Somebody gave him a drink and one can only presume that somebody else—probably one of the guests—suggested he should stay to dinner. At any rate his presence was otherwise quite overlooked until the middle of the meal when he was observed closely examining his bread plate through an eyeglass.

"I say—dammit," he exclaimed, "this is Mess stuff. How the . . ."

But no one paid the slightest attention, least of all Ah Fat who, with utterly immobile features, was busy officiating with the claret. It was considered bad form to notice, let alone comment on, the means by which an overflow of guests were catered for: so far as Ah Fat was concerned the all-important consideration of "face" was involved. Later, during a very temporary lull in the hum of conversation, the same tones became audible in even more startled protest.

"I say—it's highly irregular y'know: this spoon bears the regimental crest . . ."

His further comments were quickly drowned in an immediate crescendo of talk from all sides. But it was not until the end of the meal when the Major rolled up his table napkin and found himself inserting it into a silver ring on which were engraved his initials and the date of his christening way back in the dim 'eighties, that his eyeglass fell out altogether and he left the party rather hurriedly in a mood of bewildered mutterings.

Following a short period of relaxation after dinner on these occasions, we frequently indulged in a thoroughly destructive, but invariably hilarious game which was known as "Fanning the Disc". There was a certain amount of ritual about the pre-liminaries, rather like the prologue to a bull fight: first, a procession of house-coolies came into our wide lounge and solemnly moved all the chairs and sofas close to the walls, then turned all the tables on their sides and piled them up in front of the window. Lots would then ceremoniously be drawn for places behind the various barricades of furniture, leaving one unfortunate, known as "The Tosser" high and dry in the middle of the room. Presently Ah Fat would make his entrance, clutching to his stomach a vast pile of sing-song girl gramo-phone records which it was his duty to purchase in the native city at the equivalent cost of about threepence a piece: these he placed in the centre of the floor, and, having bobbed his head three times at "The Tosser", retreated and, while making his dignified exit through the door, moved over the switch which turned on the large four-bladed ceiling-fan to full. The rest of the proceedings need hardly require description, except to say they were based on the principle of musical chairs. When "The Tosser" shouted "hup" and lobbed a record neatly into the whirling tornado above, those behind the barricades had to scramble one place to the right and he, in turn, dived for one of the covers before the next man got there. Apart from the discs which naturally finished in smithereens, quite a lot of other things used to get broken as well, but oddly enough there were never any serious casualties amongst personnel. One boisterous and evergreen naval captain thought it was the greatest fun he had experienced since his gun-room days, until it came his turn to stand under the fan armed with a disc and shout "hup": he then made one leap for the door and, flinging himself through it, collapsed in a heap on the top of Ah Fat, who, having acquired a baseball catcher's head-piece, had been witnessing his proceedings through one of the glass panels.

It may be as well, perhaps, in some ways, but it is still none the less an unhappy thought to reflect that at the dictates of condition and restriction there is probably nowhere in the world to-day where the natural exuberance of youth in quite harmless measure can be allowed a loose rein. At least I hope that in certain regimental Messes all the young officers of this era are not too serious minded to let off a bit of steam after dinner on guest nights. It is good, in the days when one settles down, especially in an atmosphere of essential austerity charged with so many uneasy doubts, to feel, as mayhap the rising generation never will feel, that at least one has had one's measure of fun out of life. I wonder: are visiting Majors still prone to be de-bagged nor allow their dignity to diminish the fun . . .? but I'm digressing. I just had in mind to relate an occasion when in a certain army Mess in North China we indulged in a series of set scrums with a strangely unsuitable article to serve as a ball, before proceeding to an even more vigorous and discomforting pastime known as "highcock-alorum". I know it sufficed to split my boiled shirt round the neck, and that some cheerful idiot immediately saw fit to insert his finger into the aperture and transform the split into a formidable rent: after that my shirt was anybody's: indeed I think everyone claimed his fair portion of it. The matter was not only one of distress, but of obvious concern, to Ah Fat, who, shortly before seven the next morning followed me out to the *Mafoo* who was pacifying my rather impatient pony by the gate, and remarked:

"Masta—me no savvy at all, at all."

"What thing, Ah Fat?" I asked abruptly, suppressing some tendency towards a liver.

"Me no savvy," he insisted in perplexed tones. "Masta come home last ni': collar and tie b'long all ploper—same time Masta no have shirt . . ."

Shortly I was jumping the narrow creeks and galloping round the grave mounds in the open country. My liver was restored and I could put my head back and laugh in the crisp air and the early red sun. This was a *great* life and indeed it was worth the living.

Ah Fat was a servant who, though he could never fathom what it was all about, came none the less to adapt himself in a full-hearted manner to the many and varied peculiarities and pastimes of the foreigner: he was there, and indeed obviously happy to be there, with the sole object of rendering never-questioning fealty in all circumstances and conditions. At the same time, even if his very presence had not demanded it, his dignity was always our most essential consideration and the preservation of his Face, which to him was paramount, was never absent from the thoughts of those who were privileged to come into touch with him. I paid him the equivalent of thirty-six pounds a year, which, added to his recognised per-quisites and the fact that he lived on "soup-meat", made him a positive "Croesus" in his native environment. Even he, with rather more fervour than that demanded by the elegancies, frequently protested that he was overpaid.

Overpaid! Compare the picture of average present-day

England with the one typical example of a dozen cosmopolitans, after several sets of tennis, seated round a table on the verandah of the famous Circle Sportif Français in Shanghai, playing liar dice for the distinction of signing the chit for the next drink. At, say, nine o'clock one generously suggests they all come home and dine; whereupon the Head Club Boy is called and the information is relayed on the telephone to Ah Fat to the effect that twelve guests will be arriving for dinner in half an hour's time. Ah Fat knows the form, weighs up his immediate stock of food and cutlery against requirements, and then enquires who his Master's immediate companions at the French Club may be. On being informed, he puts through a series of swift calls on his own account and by the time the guests have arrived and partaken of a "cock-a-tail" the banquet is served. Familiar plate, though it be not one's own; a recognition of some delicacy which could only have emerged from the refrigerator of Mrs. S. who is sitting next to you; a Vice-Consul's own Boy, pushing in an unfamiliar chair for him: all these things were more than likely to happen, and though they were noticed, no mention was ever made concerning them: they were accepted as being inevitable in a community which lived freely and where highly-trained service was considered, by those who undertook it, to be both an honourable and an enviable profession to follow.

I shall not easily forget one final episode which may justify revival here. It happened shortly after I was married and I think my wife has in more recent years frequently been fortified, if not encouraged, by the recollection of it as she stands over the sink peeling the potatoes and, devoid of much hope, ponders over the possibilities of their eventual accompaniment

on the table being mildly palatable, or even existent. We had
asked six people to tiffin on a Sunday to eat the snipe I had shot
a few days earlier; I arrived very late from the golf course
unexpectedly accompanied by my opponent, which made nine
of us in all. My wife, quite new to such irregularities, took the
earliest opportunity to express considerable concern in a somewhat agitated undertone.

"Darling—you've made it nine: what shall we do?"

"About what?"

"Well, darling—you were only clever enough to shoot eight
snipe . . ."

"Oh, that's all right," I reassured her, feeling slightly self-
conscious. "Does Ah Fat know?"

Ah Fat knew all right, and in due course he delicately offered
round nine perfect-looking snipe on a large platter to each in
turn, coming to me last. He must have juggled that platter
about with no mean dexterity to make certain that no one
among the others helped themselves to the "bird" which was
intended for me. I think he must have hewn it out of buffalo
hide with a chisel: but the *pièce de résistance* about it was the
beak, which had been carved out of a wooden skewer and
tinted with soya-bean oil. But nobody else knew the difference.

One of the amazing things about Ah Fat was the fact that I
never knew him suffer a day's illness: also, I suppose because
in common with the majority of his fellow countrymen he
could sleep at all times wherever or whenever opportunity
offered, he was never the slightest bit dismayed at being summoned to cook bacon and eggs at the most unearthly hours.
It was a thoroughly unequal struggle to try and persuade him
to take a holiday and visit his children and grandchildren in

Ningpo-more-far at that native festival of re-union—Chinese New Year. "Make plenty trouble", was his invariable rejoinder to the suggestion. He insisted only on two hours off once a fortnight to keep his appointment at the establishment he termed "the wash-body shop", and I can only presume it was no subterfuge, for he was in every sense always most immaculately clean.

He was there in the crowd on the landing stage against the Shanghai Bund that saw the passengers, my wife and I among them, embark on the tender which was to sever my own happy ten-year-long sojourn as an unimportant "trader-guest" of no particular consequence in his country. I was more moved by that personal parting than by saying good-bye to any of the Europeans or Americans who formed the more disinterested pattern of one's business and social life. They were grand people, but in their cosmopolitan atmosphere of gaiety we should soon be forgotten, and none of them possessed that true genius for friendship and affection which I knew was deeply embedded in the heart of Ah Fat. As the tender slipped her moorings and he stood there immobile and impervious to the milling crowd that jostled about him, I observed for the first and only time in our long association that he was capable of visible emotion. And it touched me to the extent of hopelessly wishing I could leap ashore and thank him all over again. Instead, I thought I must make perhaps no more than a vain effort to comfort and distract him. Cupping my hands to my mouth I bawled to him across the widening water, "Ah Fat!"

He looked up and I saw that his lips were just capable of framing the inevitable, "Yes, Masta."

"Look-see Custom's clock. Ah Fat's time-piece no right!"

I hoped it might serve to lighten a situation that was mutually tense.

He fumbled under his gown and I saw him produce his infallible token of reliability: he glanced at it, then up to the Customs' tower, put the watch to his ear, then, ripping it from its strap hurled it over the heads of the crowd into the swirling wash of the Whang-po river. Then his face lit up again and his features were restored to a broad grin. It was a magnificent gesture since he undoubtedly knew, as I did, that the Customs' clock was invariably eight minutes fast. But I sent him a much better watch from London—a self-winding affair—to wear on his wrist.

His letter concludes, "Time-piece plenty long day go now— no savvy how to stop—s'pose no stop, Ah Fat die too soon— what thing?" So now that I am no more than a memory to him it seems that he has centred his destinies at the dictates of my gift. He remains rich in a sublime and simple faith of which I well might wish to have been more deserving.

.　.　.　.　.　.

VIII

"TALLY HO"

Some time ago I visited a large industrial works in the North
of England where I was shown something of the produc-
tion, packing and despatch for export, of a crude chemical
which, as an essential raw material is sold in profusion all over
the world.

I watched the gunny bags being machine-marked, then saw
them automatically filled and stitched before they passed along
a moving platform to be mechanically tallied into a barge. The
craft, with three others like it, would shortly be making passage
along two rivers and a canal; and then another consignment of
a thousand tons would be ready for transhipment into an
ocean-going vessel in Liverpool docks.

"I hear they *eat* this stuff in China," remarked the foreman:
"what d'you know about that?"

"Precious little," I replied: "though I believe the Cantonese
do use it in certain types of native confectionery. Myself, I'm
better acquainted with the customs of the North," I went on,
"where, although they don't actually *eat* it—not at any rate in
its present form—they certainly consume it in a wide variety
of other ways."

The foreman looked slightly disillusioned, as though a good
story he had been telling for years had suddenly come a trifle
unstuck. He proceeded on a different tack.

"I s'pose without any of this modern equipment—devices and such-like as we've got here—your old Chinaman would take maybe a week to discharge this lot."

"A week!" I laughed. "A mere thousand tons . . ."

My mind slipped back through the years and I found myself reflecting on the vivid atmosphere of that festival in North China known as "Cargo-come" day.

.   .   .   .

Mr. Ho—nearly six foot and over seventeen stone of him—stood framed in the open doorway of the District Manager's office in Tientsin. He was head custodian of the Company's extensive Godowns on the South bank of the Pei-ho, and, since he professed to speak no English, I was doing my best to explain to him in his own tongue that I would be on parade at 6.30 hours the following morning to witness the discharge of a thousand tons *Yung Gi-en* (literally—Foreign Powder) from lighters to store. Mr. Ho understood: that wise and loyal old character understood a lot of things about which he said but little.

At the appointed hour next day, I find that the hatch covers have been removed from three lighters moored alongside our property and several gangs, comprising about a hundred coolies in all, are standing by. Mr. Ho, surrounded by stacks of bamboo sticks and with parcels of coppers and small silver spread out on a table before him, sits in his accustomed place by the open Godown door. The stage is all set for the performance of an arduous task made lighter through its accompaniment by all the fun of the fair.

Soon, two long processions of scantily-clad coolies, each with a two-hundredweight bag perched across his shoulders, are moving along the gang-planks, then over the dusty pathway to converge at the Warehouse entrance through which, as they pass, each receives from the hand of Mr. Ho a plain foot-long bamboo stick. These toilers are the "Individualists" who, on the completion of five such journeys and the acquisition of the same number of plain bamboos, exchange them for a single one of slightly larger dimensions and decorated with a red band. As soon as twenty-five individual journeys have been completed and five of the larger embellished sticks acquired, Mr. Ho then recovers them in exchange for the agreed rate of piece-work hire: and the recipient, with a bit of "the ready" tucked away in his waist-band can now afford to take a well-earned breather.

At the same time a third procession, of a somewhat different order, is emanating from the remaining lighter and also converging at the Godown entrance to claim the attentions of Mr. Ho. It is composed of the more sporting get-rich-quick element who operate in pre-arranged pairs and, with the aid of a pole and a sling, carry between them three bags at a time, to the accompaniment of the appropriate sing-song chant. Though he must accept them (like foreigners and death) as being inevitable, Mr. Ho is wont to take a dim view of these duet-performers since, wise though he may be, he has never succeeded in discovering how to divide three into five, and remains strongly averse to the necessity of adjusting his system to meet special arrangements. He is also somewhat of a rarity in that he is a Chinese born without a natural instinct to gamble; and holds but small regard for chanting team-mates in general,

who subsequently draw lots to decide which of them becomes
entitled to cash-in the collectively-earned sticks and retain the
more legal form of tender. In particular, he is possessed of still
less sympathy towards the Unfortunate, who, having sweated
and strained an hour or so to no more than his friend's advantage, is now obliged to start afresh, "humping" among the
"Individualists".

With a nice sense of timing—that is when it may be calculated that Mr. Ho has recovered sufficient length of bamboo to
have been fairly active with the disbursements—the scene
becomes enlivened by the arrival of a succession of one-man
portable establishments. These are broken down to enable
them to be borne in two nicely-balanced sections dangling from
either end of a long pole slung across the shoulder. Presently
they are set up on some convenient pitch in the shape of
General Emporium, Chow Shop and Kitchen combined, and,
of course, the complete Tonsorial Parlour. They comprise the
more honest traders: but inevitably appearing in their wake,
and bent on getting amongst the money, come those of lesser
repute: the letter-writers, the magicians, the story-tellers, the
jugglers, the hand-spring artistes, and several others representative of the native element among spivs and oppor-
tunists. Consequently as the morning wears on, the scene
of activity in front of our Godown becomes more and more
diverse.

But far from troubling him, the fair-ground atmosphere
surrounding his coolie-hire is welcomed by Mr. Ho. He knows
that Chinese casual labour becomes as the lilies of the field, in
that it toils not, when it has a few coppers to spin. The cavalcade
about us serves the purpose of attracting a large portion of up-

to-date earnings, thereby necessitating an immediate resumption of work by those who otherwise would be too inclined to classify themselves as the idle rich. So it all aids towards discharge being completed with sufficient despatch to avoid payment of demurrage on the lighters: this consideration, coupled with minor concern over the accuracy of his tally, represents the sum total of Mr. Ho's worries.

The Chow-vendor has staked out a claim and already his soup and rice pans are bubbling and steaming away behind him, while his bowls and other utensils are laid out for hire, as required, before him. Meanwhile, in the manner of a rumba musician, he is engaged in shaking ten chop-sticks up and down in a wooden cylinder: this not only serves to draw the attentions of the multitude to the appetising aromas of his kitchen, but affords the hungry an opportunity of extracting the stick which has a well-defined chip about its unseen end, and which allows the lucky ones the privilege of eating "on the house".

Some distance away a sartorially elegant clothier is beating a tattoo, then giving voice concerning his display of coolie cloth and drawing attention to the nimble skill of his cut. A white-bearded patriarch has erected two poles from which hang a score of bird-cages housing a complete aviary of songsters in all sizes and dressed in a wide variety of plumage, all of whom appear to be contributing a fair share to the general cacophony. Further along, a more lugubrious-looking type is sounding a funeral gong and accepting first premiums on insurance against the inevitable expense of one's obsequies. There, in oddly-assorted array, stand the pea-nut seller, the fruit merchant, the black-egg specialist, and the professor with the patent medicines. Business is brisk all round and the brisker it becomes so much more speedily does the main operation proceed and so much better pleased is Mr. Ho.

The Barber, traditionally recognised among the Chinese as belonging to the lowest caste of all, has, appropriately enough, opened up his saloon adjacent to the temporarily-erected latrines, and is now engaged upon the task of shaving heads at the rate of half a dozen an hour. Now and again his chair is occupied by a customer who requires a little additional attention, such as a pummelling of the back, a little massage on the stomach, or perhaps just a touch of chiropody. For, despite his low status in the social order, the Chinese Barber serves a versatile apprenticeship and furthermore adheres to a fixed tariff, with none of your tossing for double or nothing, as practised in the other professions: maybe he finds it too risky when he never knows beforehand what he may be called upon to deal with next.

We move about in an animated, not uncolourful, atmosphere amid sounds of clamour and song and an overall spirit, carefree in luck and philosophical in misfortune, that, on the whole, seems to breathe an air of happiness. We are amongst those the great majority of whom are indeed content to live for the day and very much hand to mouth: they are disinterested in political crises and oblivious to changing ideologies: they are not bothered by Union regulations and have never been introduced to a Shop Steward. They live without the obligation of responsibilities and eventually they die without any knowledge of the fear of death: all of which would appear to breed a strange contentment. There are the unpleasantries in season, of course, such as hunger and cold; but usually, not far distant, there's sufficient "humping" to be found that will ward off both dis-comforts. Sickness—well, if you're too sick to work and there's no copper-cash in the kitty, then, logically, you're much better off if you're dead.

In the fullness of time the reformers will change all this—one must hope they will: but it is a simple philosophy that dies hard, and deprived of it, with a host of "rights" in substitution, one earnestly hopes that the lovable character that is the care-free coolie, will continue to reap his reward of contentment.

Let us take a glance at Fu Sung as an example of his kind and calling: he is happy indeed, for this has been a day of days for him—so far. From being penniless at dawn, he has since cashed-in the ringed bamboos at the expense of team-mate Wang Er; and has added to this success by selecting the chop stick with the chipped end. He has received double pay for no more than an hour's work, filled his belly free of charge, had his head shaved and a corn cut out of his toe, slept peacefully for an hour and is still some thirty cents and a few copper-cash in hand: furthermore he has just supplemented his earnings by joining a school of squatters near the water's edge and winning two hands of Fan-tan. But if, as one strongly suspects will be the case, he allows himself shortly to be drawn towards battling his wits against those of the travelling "catchee-lady" trickster (with the inevitable result) he will philosophically adopt the adage of Kipling and, not breathing a word about his loss, start again at his beginnings: in other words, he'll get down to a bit more "humping" as an "Individualist".

We find by mid-afternoon that former team-mate and co-chanter, Wang Er, has atoned for his luckless start and, having eaten, is now sleeping peacefully in a spot of shade. He has also discharged an obligation, in that for the sum of five copper-cash he has dictated a letter to the travelling scribe which will serve to notify his aged mother in far-away Hunan that, although he has indeed recently been appointed a partner in the Transport and Haulage business, he finds himself in no immediate position to subscribe towards her coffin fund. Wang Er's prevailing weakness for Face-building is invariably landing him in jams of this sort with his somewhat gullible and ever-opportunist parent. Then, as he awakens, his conscience no doubt stirs him into an immediate resumption of "humping": at least he should carry sufficient number of bags to supply his letter with a postage stamp and so spare his mother the expense of delivery fees in addition to her subsequently being called upon to finance the doubtful satisfaction of having her son's communication read to her. Also he is possessed of a purely transitory fancy that he might start saving something up . . .

Well—we've stolen glances at Fu Sung and Wang Er: there's not much that differs in character or feature among the other ninety-eight who work and idle in rotation, at the dictates of fancy or sheer necessity. Time is getting on now and it will be worth while seeing how Mr. Ho is faring in his battle against it.

I put the question to him and while continuing to juggle his bamboos with his right hand, the fingers of his left perform a startling operation on the abacus. Mr. Ho then transfers his glance from some Chinese hieroglyphics scrawled on a scrap of paper before him and casts his eyes towards the sun.

"Another one thousand, four hundred and thirty-odd bags to discharge in two hours and ten minutes," he announces with assured exactitude. There is no need for me to ask him whether or when he intends to introduce a "Hit or Miss" session, or whether it might be more economical to pay a limited amount of demurrage on the lighters. By his own peculiar methods he will have the respective merits of every alternative already weighed up, and at five o'clock, with an hour and a half in hand, he will take the course guaranteed to serve the best interests of all.

"Hit or Miss" tactics, when employed, are much akin to a sporting declaration in cricket, where the opposing side is given a limited time in which to go for the runs or lose the match. Mr. Ho would loudly proclaim for the benefit of all and sundry at the appropriate moment that there were yet nine hundred and sixty-eight bags to discharge and seventy-four minutes within which to complete it: bamboo sticks worth double if accomplished—otherwise quite valueless.

The effect of this pronouncement is electrifying: recumbent bodies spring into life from all over the place, the stalls and sideshows become suddenly deserted and games of chance are hastily abandoned. This is the best gamble of the day, and the challenge is invariably accepted with joyous acclamation.

The scene rapidly assumes the effect of a cinema film which is being projected on the screen at twice its normal speed. Long lines of laughing, shouting, good-humoured coolies jostle each other as they double under their burdens and then speed back for more. Mr. Ho, with a box of bamboos between his knees, is handing out the sticks so fast that he takes on the appearance of a normally sedate 'cello player who has suddenly gone berserk. Only his assistants, perched on high within and hard-pressed to maintain stacking uniformity under such rapid fire from below, are reluctant participators in this win-or-burst

effort. The lighter-hands don't care much about it either: they
are feeding the remaining bags on to a long queue of impatient
backs with such dexterity that, from the middle distance, they
appear as a well-drilled squad performing physical jerks at
lightning speed. But Mr. Ho will see that full recompense is
paid to all: and before instituting "Hit-or-Miss" sessions he is
invariably aware that the balance is weighed heavily in favour
of double rates, but only over a period calculated to cost less
than the price of delay to the lighters. As I remarked earlier,
Mr. Ho is not a betting man and only indulges these practices
in the interests of sound economy and also because everyone is
happy in the end. Everyone except perhaps the salesmen and
spivs who, like a travelling circus, strike camp at the first cry
of "Hit or Miss" and waddle away towards fresh fields with
their emporiums and saloons slung across their shoulders: Mr.
Ho is sure they have done well enough—a view that is shared,
though rapidly forgotten, by a vast multitude of others.

Then finally, when the shouting and the tumult has died and
all except Mr. Ho have departed, I approach him as he remains
seated there in the cool of the evening, gently perspiring but
quite undefeated as he neatly stacks away his bamboos in
readiness for some future festival of "Cargo-come".

"*Hao fa-tze*," I announce, meaning in the English idiom,
"Good show", then add with only mild apprehension, "How
does it all work out?"

Mr. Ho seems slightly perplexed.

"Only nine thousand, nine hundred and ninety-eight bags,
including five that broke in the lighters," he proclaims sorrow-
fully. "There must be two more somewhere."

I suppress my utter amazement at this miracle of tallying

which Mr. Ho invariably accomplishes with accuracy, aided by no more than two sets of sticks, the beads of his abacus and an amount of money left over in odd bits of newspaper which serve as his till.

"Two whole bags missing!" I observe in mock horror. "The trouble with you, Mr. Ho," I add in effect, "is that your ideas of making a tally are hopelessly out of date. I hear they have a machine at the Works in England—they call it 'the magic eye'; we'll have to see about getting one sent out: we just can't afford to go on losing two bags out of every ten thousand you know. It's not good enough."

Mr. Ho, whose sense of humour is far more subtle than mine, undoubtedly catches the look in my eye, but he does not yet know that I have his ace tucked away in my pocket. So I allow him to express himself volubly and at considerable length on the subject of all "devil" machines which in his view are not only thoroughly unreliable, but are created in the West with the sole purpose of maliciously discrediting the far more elegant and accurate methods of the East. "Those two bags," he concludes, "could never have come up the river."

"You are perfectly right, as usual," I assure him quietly. "To a humble Westerner like myself the thing is quite uncanny. This piece of paper here comes from the stevedore in charge of transhipment into lighters at Taku and says 'two bags jump out of sling into bar—get drowned!' "

Mr. Ho does not smile, indeed no one has ever yet observed him to do so. But across the whole of his countenance can be detected the rich and unmistakable glow of Face preserved.

"A week!" I repeated to the foreman, "a mere thousand tons—or ten thousand bags if you like. Good heavens! In less than a day they . . . why—they'd 'eat it!' "

IX

"SHANGHAILANDER"

G LANCING back on it, I find that I have to my doubtful credit a military record, between the world wars, that must be well-nigh unique.

On leaving England for China at the end of 1923, I was placed on the Territorial Army Reserve of Officers with the rank of Lieutenant: but, through no more than the effort required to post periodic assurances of my continued existence from ten thousand miles away, I returned eleven years later to find that I had been elevated, *in absentia,* to the distinction of a Majority. This oddly-won promotion appealed to me as being all the more remarkable since it coincided with my steady descent down the non-commissioned ranks of various British Volunteer Units abroad. In Hankow, for instance, I was, for a brief spell in 1926, a Sergeant: 1930 found me in Tientsin striving to emulate such notable characters as Napoleon and Hitler, who, one is given to understand, at some time or other, also held the rank of Corporal. But two years later I was on active service adjacent to the ruins of Chapei, accoutred in a tin hat and a kilt of Hunting Stuart—and never more proud to proclaim myself—a Private soldier in the Shanghai Scottish.

The 1932 phase of "The China Incident" around the borders of the International Settlement was quite a prolonged affair, since the Japanese never anticipated that the victorious Chinese

Eighth Route Army would so valiantly stem their advances.
There was much heroism and an appalling amount of destruc-
tion accomplished by both sides. As far as we members of the
Shanghai Volunteer Corps were concerned, we had ringside
seats at the contest and a lot of time away from our offices.
The only real scare I had was the occasion on which I assayed
to climb into the ring itself for an even closer view of the
exchanges.

During long hours of standing on guard at the very fringe of
the Settlement boundary, I had come to be on quite amiable
terms with the Japanese sentry on the other side of the barbed
wire. Our affinity could not be described as being much more
than a nodding acquaintanceship, interspersed with a few deep
bows as occasion appeared to demand, since conversation was
limited to a few irrelevant words in each other's tongue. This
was, of course, before the days when Japanese sentries delighted
to embarrass the Englishman by inviting him to remove his
nether garments: and in any case the diminutive "Ko-ko San",
as I called him, was every inch a gentleman. Whenever I came
on duty he would remove his coal-scuttle of a tin hat and
incline his body gracefully in my direction. When the Sergeant
who had posted me was safely round the corner I always
returned the compliment with an extravagant gesture: and
Ko-ko San, who I came to the conclusion was never relieved,
expressed his pleasure by drawing in an audible breath through
his protruding teeth. On a seemingly quiet day I intimated to
him that I would appreciate the opportunity of exploring the
world that lay on his side of the fence, and Ko-ko San readily
obliged by heaving back a solid mass of International wire and
invited me through. I afforded him the compliment of raising

my tin hat to him and then passed out of his view down what I thought was a deserted alley-way. My exploration was but short-lived before a sharp rat-tat-tat behind me automatically and instantly caused me to hurl my body into a prone position on to the floor of a burnt-out grain shop. Shortly I heard it again and I could only presume that it was a machine-gun firing spasmodically from further down the street; and, since I had made use of such convenient cover, I supposed, with a slight feeling of relief, that I was not the particular target which was claiming its attentions. Then unexpectedly there was another burst, followed by a much louder bang, considerably closer at hand but emanating from the other direction: and I concluded that the thing must be some form of mobile weapon. I was perfectly correct, for after a suitable interval I rose from the floor, drew the hem of my Hunting Stuart closer about me and cautiously cocked an eye round the door. The narrow street was quite deserted, save for a solitary Japanese officer who was experiencing obvious difficulty in starting up his motor cycle.

It served as suitable admonishment to a foolhardy "Shanghai-lander" who had temporarily deserted his post to satisfy a morbid curiosity: and I returned hurriedly and rather shame-facedly to the obsequious Ko-ko San who bowed me back into my own province.

The only other occasion during that particular "war" on which I was shaken—and I mean literally shaken—was when I was having lunch, during a brief respite from duty, in the dining-room situated on the top storey of the Palace Hotel. The whole building suddenly swayed to and fro in an alarming manner as though caused by a violent earth tremor; and then we heard a dull subterranean roar. A handful of Chinese patriots in a sampan loaded down with high explosives had just endeavoured to blow up the Japanese battle-cruiser *Idzumo* moored just beyond the Garden Bridge two hundred yards away: but alas, through some error in the timing arrangements had only succeeded in annihilating themselves without trace. Fortunately one did not have time to reflect until later that all the miniature skyscrapers along the Shanghai Bund are built on the swamp which, many decades earlier, the Chinese authorities of the time had blandly allocated to the "Foreign Devils" as being the most suitable *locale* wherein they might be permitted to create a settlement of their own.

During the remainder of that particular state of emergency I thought it expedient to exercise the precaution of taking my meals at street level.

After the polite Ko-ko San and his comrades withdrew from the ruins of Chapei and the native districts surrounding the Settlement, and the state of emergency being temporarily over, I sent my Hunting Stuart to the cleaners, and, one evening, betook myself with others on a tour of the "battlefields". The heaviest and fiercest engagement had been fought over the Chinese racecourse at Kiangwan, where everything was flattened and burnt save for a slightly-charred and generously-riddled notice board that stood, as it were registering mute protest, in the midst of the wasteland that was no longer encircled by the wide sweep of gleaming white rails. Still clearly discernible, in English and Chinese characters, it bore the strict injunction "No Shooting Allowed. By Order". Yet so readily adaptable are the tireless enthusiasts who follow the

Sport of Kings that we were again disarmingly spotting the losers there within the month.

.　　.　　.　　.　　.　　.

With the possible exception of the French Foreign Legion, the Shanghai Volunteer Corps, recruited from all sections of its community for the protection of the International Settlement must, in its time, have been the most cosmopolitan company of assorted soldiery to be found anywhere in the world. The Commanding Officer was a Regular British Army Colonel whose appointment was sponsored by the War Office: and, in my day, the Adjutant was a gallant and immaculate gentleman who had been seconded to the Unit from the Scots Guards. So far as I am aware, no other regular soldiers of any nationality were employed on the strength. The second-in-command, during my service with the Corps, was a Portuguese business man and the Headquarters Staff was composed of a rare diversity in race and colour, all of whom combined admirably to maintain an efficient and well-trained body of men.

My mind now begins to boggle as I endeavour to recollect the individual units which comprised the Corps, for they were in great number and variety. In pride of place on ceremonial occasions, such as the Annual March Past, invariably came the cavalry: this consisted of the American Troop, who sat astride their Chinese ponies garbed in "Mounty" hats; and the British Light Horse, perhaps naturally composed of the younger element among the racing and hunting community. The squadron of mounted Englishmen invariably looked resplendent with spurs to their boots and chain-mail burnished about their shoulders: second only, of course, to the Shanghai Scottish, they lent a great deal of colour as well as a high level of smart bearing to all ceremonial parades. I am sure it was altogether a gross injustice to their habits that some jealous wit of a foot-slogger had once thought fit to dub them "The Tight Horse"—but inevitably the name stuck!

Then came the companies of Infantry: the English contingent which included in its ranks one or two Chinese who rightly claimed to be British because they were born in Hong Kong: the Americans bearing their fire-arms on the wrong shoulder and swinging their own arms across their stomachs; the Portuguese, rather diminutive and dark-skinned; the Filipinos, still more diminutive and even darker-skinned; the Chinese company, all bespectacled and with a tendency to break into the goose-step; the Russians, even in Shanghai summer, with their great-coats neatly furled about them: and then, bravest of all, preceded by pipers in plaid and plume, invariably raising the biggest cheer from the region of the saluting base, came the swinging sporrans and pipe-clayed spats of the Shanghai Scottish—three score more of kilted exiles from their father's land.

It may be that among those sixty or so there was an occasional strain of the pure Sassenach: but our Company Commander was a tolerant man who raised no particular objection if Mr. St. George Tudor was a fine specimen of manhood and fancied himself within the folds of a Hunting Stuart. He drew the line, however, at applications from Filipinos or Portuguese who claimed Highland ancestry and legend has it, was once politely but firmly regretful to a Chinese cook who explained hopefully that his father had been connected with the laundry business in Scotland Road, Liverpool.

Some of our recruits showed themselves up rather badly on their first appearance in the drill hall after being fitted out. The one with a name something like Llewellyn Jones, who fell-in proudly wearing his sporran over his apron was admonished only slightly less than the man who came on parade in apron only, having considered it correct on such occasions to leave his kilt at home.

So much for the Shanghai Scottish, and I hope that I have not omitted to mention any remaining units of infantry. I do not recall a Japanese Company, and there were certainly no French or German outfits. When the various foreign concessions in Shanghai were merged into one International Settlement, the French alone preferred to remain aloof, maintaining their own clearly-defined extra-territorial boundaries. Thus their nationals were not eligible, at any rate as a body, to join the corps which was entirely an International Settlement affair. During the early 1930's the Germans were already to be observed clad in brown shirts and banded with swastikas, raising their arms and "Sieg heil"-ing rather surreptitiously among their own somewhat remote community.

Bringing up the rear of the parade, following the Foot-sloggers, were the "Fancy-chaps". The Armoured Car Company was the most imposing and apparently the best-equipped of these Auxiliary Units. There were odd collections of light artillery, sappers, signallers, cyclists and the inevitable hangers-on who only turned out on Inspection Day. But most remarkable of all was the unit formed in 1933 who called themselves the Air Detachment. They wore forage caps, riding breeches and tunics which came right across the breast and hooked at the sides in the precise pattern of those favoured by the original

Royal Flying Corps. I do not know how many of them had ever flown, let alone piloted an aircraft, though I imagine such qualifications were unnecessary since the Shanghai Volunteers did not boast so much as a captive balloon. In fact it was always very much of a mystery to us "outsiders" what functions the Air Detachment *did* perform. Whenever I was bold enough to put the question to the chap who sat next to me in the office, who was a "founder-member" of the thing, he invariably came over all coy and intimated that it was all terribly "hush-hush". But he looked very nice in his uniform!

In addition to the Inspection and March Past, there was another annual affair in the curriculum of the Shanghai Volunteers which produced a sense of rivalry and called for a great deal of earnest preparation. It was the inter-unit competition, adjudicated by the General Officer Commanding the British Garrison in China, to decide which was the smartest, most efficient all-round Company or Squadron of the whole Corps.

Though we "Shanghailanders" were always determined to take this opportunity of proving, through a generous display of all that was best in soldierly-like qualities, that we were second to none: the fact must be recorded that—try as we certainly did —we never, in my time, won the trophy; neither, for that matter, did any of the other British or American units.

What happened was all the more remarkable to me since in the course of my earlier wanderings through the interior of North China I frequently found myself in the vicinity of some native garrison: and it had amused me to witness the ill-equipped rabble of some rising War-lord undergoing their military exercises. They would not, I feel sure, be lacking in courage but in appearance and drill they suggested a mob of overgrown slum-children playing at soldiers on a waste plot of land. In those days, before China was faced with a common foe, and prior to the beginnings of the prolonged struggle between the "Nationalist" and "Liberation" armies, no one took China's frequent civil wars with any great degree of seriousness: least of all, no doubt, the bulk of participants themselves who probably knew, to a lesser extent even than anyone else, what might be the cause of the conflict. The conflict itself invariably consisted of no more than a few day's skirmishing before the inevitable buying and selling of troops began: and, as a consequence, the swashbuckling Commander, who had drained the resources of the local peasantry to greater effect and the better advantage of his war-chest, was invariably in a position to proclaim himself the victor: and then everyone went home to tea.

By this time it may be gathered that the discipline and efficiency of Chinese soldiers, in those comparatively recent days could serve no very good purpose and was therefore of little account: and this, in turn, makes it all the more remarkable to reflect on the fact that the inter-unit competition of the Shanghai Volunteer Corps, with an almost Guards-like standard of exacting demand, was always, or nearly always, won—and deservedly so—by the Company of Infantry which was officered and manned throughout by Chinese.

With the abandonment of extra-territorial rights throughout China there are now no longer—save in the Colony of Hong Kong—anytrained military units of foreign volunteers. Like so many other institutions in a changing world, their being is, at least to me, no more than a memory that is mingled with pride and good-fellowship, interspersed in a single instance with grave humiliation.

But perhaps it is as well, now, to forget how in the early days of 1927 the British Volunteers in Hankow, at the instigation of a higher authority, were ordered to surrender their arms and equipment, the Concessional territory they had been formed to protect, and the last vestiges of British prestige on the Yangtze. We thought rather fiercely at the time, that we should not have been denied the opportunity to fight for these things: yet though the incident may be out of date and forgotten, I shall always remember the expression on the face of our Commanding Officer—normally a staid and charming Scottish doctor—as he dismissed us for the last time and then savagely ripped off his much be-medalled tunic.

But I prefer to reflect on the spirit and simplicity in all units whereby, for instance, an officer or non-commissioned officer who was not popular, or not efficient, or who merely felt that it was someone else's turn, found his way back into the ranks. I had the experience, which must indeed be the envy of many past and present members of the regular and irregular forces, in finding that my appointment as Sergeant coincided with the reversion of the Sergeant-major to the ranks of my platoon. I shall continue to think, too, of my inability to find the solution to a particularly vexing problem in the office upon the outcome of which the success of my future career in commerce might well be staked. Just when I felt most hopelessly baffled and foresaw myself as a seedy, middle-aged failure, the sirens over the Power Company started wailing. That meant a state of emergency had arisen and the Volunteers were being called out immediately, which left me just enough time to explain the essentials of the problem to my elderly chief and make a dash, in timely relief, for the Drill Hall.

Above all I shall continue to reflect on the gallant comradeship of the "Shanghailanders" and all the units abroad to which I once proudly belonged. But my final salute must be afforded to that great company of Chinese business clerks who moulded themselves into the pattern that might well be seen within the railings of Wellington Barracks and which rightly won the respect and envious admiration of the rest of us, who were never quite a match for their model.

X

TRAVEL-AMAH

"MARIE", who travelled more than twenty thousand miles with us, was a transient element in our lives for no more than six months. But during that comparatively brief period she established herself as a vital, though often somewhat unpredictable, factor in the minds of quite a few people. The boys, as is often the way with children, are apt to retain and recall many clear-cut impressions of their travel-amah, whilst later and more established custodians of their extreme youth have faded beyond the horizon of even faint recollection. "Marie", I shall always maintain, was not only a brave doyen among Chinese nurses, holding an impartial balance between things occidental and otherwise, but she was undeniably something of a character as well.

Rather out of a blue sky I found myself called upon to spend three months in England in between my normal periods of home-leave from China: the indulgent and always generous commercial concern that employed me were gracious enough to insist that I should be accompanied by my wife and our, then three-year-old, twin sons and, far more importantly, made it financially possible for me to do so. The Travel-Amah was however my personal liability, but I offset the outlay for her passage and pay as an investment likely to extend to my wife and myself that dividend of freedom aboard a large passenger liner which hitherto both of us had appreciated in full measure —but only as separate entities. We assured ourselves that, having hitherto travelled suchwise only as eligible individuals, under rare and ever romantic skies, it would be pleasantly interesting to enjoy such a break together: subconsciously we may also have harboured a secret wish to steal a glimpse at each other's form under the restricting handicap of a mutually happy union.

At all events it was in answer to an advertisement inserted in the vernacular press that "Marie" rolled up, in a lacquer-glossed private ricksha, at our house in Shanghai, a week before we were due to sail via Suez. In accordance with the age-old custom of her country, she presumably paid the requisite toll to the house-boy, then delivered herself of a few well-chosen ancestral elegancies to the resident Amah before being permit-ted entry to the presence of the Master and Missy. She was launched upon us as my wife and I were relaxing over an exclusively-marital Martini and—since such was the life in Shanghai in those days—reflecting how many evenings had elapsed since we had previously looked forward to dining à deux at home.

"Me come: look-see: by-n-by maybe go."

It was a statement much akin to that more famous one uttered by Julius Caesar at the successful conclusion of his Pontic campaign and well-nigh as all-embracing. In "Marie's" case it was accompanied by the intermittent flash of gold teeth and a positive tintinnabulation that emerged from a score of thin silver bangles. The "bun" of her hair was adorned by a single white bloom, while the lobes of her ears were hung with jade. And she wore a flowered-silk gown, modelled in the

Chinese style, which as though in compensation for its high severity of neckline, was slit—*à la mode*—from ankle to knee.

My wife, taking comprehensive stock of this vivid intrusion upon our privacy, whilst no doubt concurrently observing a tendency on the part of her husband to whinny at it, later confessed to a first impression that our visitor must be one of the elder sisters in that somewhat elastic order of "Sing-song" sorority! It transpired, of course, that nothing could have been more remote from the truth. Though she may have bedecked herself flashily in her own social sphere, there was no adornment to lend relief to the white linen tunic and wide black trousers that henceforward became, on board and in England, the invariable rig of her working hours. She had a sense of propriety as supreme as her standards of duty and loyal affection. Thus she came to carve a special niche for herself in the Hall of Memory where, as though she were some Empress Dowager of a long-past dynasty, she remains ensconced: an unhappily now far-distant receiver of our continued respect and good-will.

But we may be forgiven if, on the occasion of our very first meeting, we were not devoid of doubts as we led her upstairs to show her the twins. They sat up abruptly in their beds, overjoyed at that hour of the evening to welcome the leanest opportunity of postponing their obligations to Morpheus: but it soon became obvious that they had discovered an instantaneous and mutual delight in each other as well.

"*Ai Ya!*" exclaimed 'Marie'. "Two piece 'allive' all-same-time!"

She was never one to appreciate economy of expression appropriate to the circumstances. Subsequently, during the first few days aboard ship, passengers observing her two identical charges were wont to stop and ask if they happened to be twins. Such enquiries invariably met with the same perplexed response. "Twilns?—no savvy 'Twilns' ", then most brightly, "Two piece 'allive' all-same-time".

The boys showed appreciation for their Travel-Amah, at their initial introduction, by jumping on their beds and treating her to a display of their acrobatic repertoire, interlaced with a few competitive feats of contortion, the whole being accompanied by wild whoops of delight. Their mother and I vainly attempted to still them but "Marie" knew the magic of the master-touch. Within moments she had them both restored within the sheets, listening wide-eyed in drowsy fascination to her soft rendering of *Sha-ke lo-tai—Shang-ke lo tai—Tung chi mah-mah Fa cha lai,* and presently they fell asleep to this crooning of an old Chinese cradle-song which, incidentally and to the bewilderment of their friends, the twins are still liable to render, in more raucous tones, to this day.

It put the matter beyond any further doubt in all our minds: "Marie" must accompany us to England. We fixed it there and then and on the strength of one more problem having solved itself, we descended the stairs and I shook up another Martini.

· · · · · ·

As we ploughed our way through the Yellow Sea a week later, with little more than a gentle pitch of the bows and a scarcely discernible thinning of attendance in the saloon at dinner, we discovered, somewhat to our consternation, that "Marie" was flying the distress signal of *mal de mer.* It reluctantly forced the conclusion upon us that if we were to experience anything less than a flat calm over the next five weeks, there would be little opportunity for my wife and me to combine forces in all, or any, of the fun and games being offered aboard. But we were quite wrong there as well: "Marie" could exert mind over matter in a most meritorious way and in no sense did she ever once lie down to her discomfort: indeed, since no milder means of persuasion could accomplish it; when she was obviously in need of rest, a gentle order became necessary to separate her from her charges. Even that was of little avail for we were eventually to discover that on such occasions she did no more than conceal herself close by, where she could still watch them without being seen.

As things turned out, if we had come aboard unequipped with a Travel-Amah, we should probably not have suffered much lack of respite from nurse-maid routine. I record this with every appreciation for "Marie's" never-failing fealty and quite dog-like devotion, adding that even had she allowed herself to be *hors de combat* for every day of the voyage it would still have been a rare privilege to have such a woman with us. But we were also privileged by the company, as fellow passengers, of a number of British Naval officers from the China Station. Two of them I must mention in particular, for they were both lovable and unforgettable characters whose close friendship we were to retain and whose subsequent careers we assiduously followed, often by devious means, during the war, right up to their ending.

One, then a post-Captain, whose name was a household word in the Navy, was destined to die as a Rear-Admiral and the Commodore of Convoys on the hazardous route to North

Russia. The other, much younger, having brought fresh lustre to no less of an honourable name, went down with the *Barham* in November, 1941. My wife and I can do no more in salute to their memory in these days than by reflecting, with pride, that we knew them: and by recalling how lost in admiration and gratitude we were for the inventive genius which they displayed in order to bring joy and ever-fresh entertainment to our sons. It was in fact amazing to witness the variety of contrivance which a post-Captain and a two-striper used to vie with each other in conjuring up for the amusement of those three-year-olds. Yet the ever-watchful "Marie" was always unobtrusively in the background.

It is impossible to forget a very rough day off the Gulf of Aden when the Old Lady in which we were travelling was pitching deep and rolling heavily with a kind of cork-screw twist which must have jarred her ageing timbers. It was no day for contrivances but undaunted by the somewhat violent motion, one twin was swinging high on a nautical leg whilst the other, clinging unsteadily to a stationary trouser-bottom, was impatiently giving tongue to imploring pleas of "Me too!" Then a sudden lurch of the ship threw the precariously-balanced two-striper off his stationary foot and the boy, then poised in forward flight, let slip his moorings and went hurtling towards the scuppers. Panic-stricken, we instinctively moved forward, fervently praying in that awful second, that the rails might save him, when "Marie" materialising from nowhere with a complexion the shade of cigar-ash, neatly fielded him with such delicate technique that he immediately came back for more. I imagine she may well have anticipated just such a happening and, regardless of the physical discomfort she was suffering, have poised herself in readiness behind an adjacent vent-shaft.

In retrospect, I have found myself reflecting upon the incident in terms of light and shade: the darker aspect concerns what might have happened if "Marie" just hadn't been there; the lighter—that were such a thing practicable, she would have qualified for a County cricket trial any day.

. . . .

"Marie" confessed, on arrival at Tilbury, that she had never seen England before. But after accepting a few preliminary differences, such as the spectacle of white men catching ropes and handling baggage, she appeared quite unmoved by any aspect of strange surroundings: evidently she was adopting the attitude of Kipling's cat to whom all places were alike.

Her wide trousers, flanked on either side by a fair-headed twin, caused little stir along Piccadilly or in Hyde Park, where many strange figures are seen at all hours of every day: but it was when I motored them North, eventually arriving at a small resort on the English side of the Solway Firth, that the locals really sat up and took notice.

My parents had taken a house for the summer near the mouth of the Firth so that they might share the company of their first grand-children in the healthy atmosphere of the sea-side. Every morning, it seemed, "Marie" was quite unable to avoid a following as she ambled out with the boys along by the gorse bushes and eventually down to the beach. There, the three of them would doodle about the sands, conversing unconcernedly together in Chinese, whilst forming the centrepiece amongst a conjecturing crowd of Cumbrian nativity. But though

"Marie", with her peculiar dignity, was indifferent to any amount of unfamiliar nods and whispers, it was by no means the case with my mother when certain implications were borne back to her via tradespeople and others such. I should explain that my mother, apart from temporary spells in warmer climes, has lived all her life in Cumberland with the natural consequence that not only she herself but almost everything that has to do with her, is widely known in the County. It was therefore a little perplexing for her to be met by a growing succession of sympathetic glances from the inhabitants and downright disturbing to learn the portent of them from one of her closest friends, who thought that the order of things created by local gossip was far more amusing than my mother did.

"They think Ronald," her friend explained between spasms of ill-concealed mirth, "has come home with a Chinese wife." Then, as if to cheer things up a bit she added, "and they are only consoled because happily the children don't look like her."

It failed to improve matters when, during the days that were left to me before I got down to work, I decided I had perhaps better forsake the golf course and be seen in the company of the twins and their more "authentic" mother. But wherever we went together, the ever-faithful "Marie" always insisted on accompanying us, walking, with that traditional deference of the native servant, a few paces to the rear, and laden down with boats and buckets, extra clothes and, more often than not, a tame and seldom-protesting duck called "Hunloke" who had come to share, with her, the boys' inseparable companionship. The sight of this rather startling procession, aided by the fact that to local ears there was no distinction between the twins' alternating addresses to "Amah" and "Mama", gave rise to the assumption that I had become even more steeped in the customs of Old Cathay and taken unto myself no less than two wives. But it was not until charabanc parties from the industrial towns of West Cumberland began pulling up at the front gate, with well-mannered demands to view "The black woman with the white children", that my mother's usual good humour showed definite signs of deterioration.

We sent for the local police sergeant who arrived on his bicycle, taking the opportunity to bear with him a somewhat faded yellow form, for completion in respect of aliens, and with which, during his thirty-odd years in the force, he had never previously been called upon to familiarise himself.

The three of us—"Marie", the Sergeant and I—sat round the dining-room table with the form of questionnaire before us, in the manner of a combined operation aimed at satisfying the regulations. The sergeant produced, then moistened with his tongue, a stub of indelible pencil, looked across at "Marie" and started, "Now—this 'ere . . .", but he made little progress further since it was soon evident that "Marie" was quite incapable of understanding a solitary word of his dialect. While he removed his helmet and mopped his brow, I picked up the blank form to see if I could improve on matters. Presently I was engaged in explaining the gist of the thing to "Marie" in her own tongue and as she rattled back the answers to me in the melodious tones of Mandarin, I caught the look in that Cumberland policeman's eye. He was leaning back in a daze wondering where on earth his pursuit of the law had now landed him: " 'eathen proceedin's reet enuff an' all" was what I felt he was longing to remark: but he satisfied himself by drawing the back of his hand across a walrus moustache and directing his attention to a bottle of beer on the sideboard.

Four bottles later we had, between us, completed the form except for the important formality of "Marie's" signature. I indicated that she inscribe it in Chinese and, to my interest, I observed her pencil-in the two characters for which the phonetic English spelling would be "Ma" and "Lee". I then realised for the first time that through the accepted tendency of the Chinese to substitute an *l* for an *r* (as in "allive" for "arrive") I had been quite mistaken in ever supposing her name to be "Marie" though, of course, to us, she always continued to remain so.

The Sergeant, now somewhat redder in the face, regarded the Chinese characters with grave misgivings, a state of affairs apparently not improved by his studying them upside down and subsequently from all angles and various distances. "T' inspector won't 'ave this," he announced solemnly. "Like, it seems to . . . well too . . ."

"Too heathen-like?" I suggested.

"Aye—that's reet enuff, Mister!" he agreed, bringing his fist down on the polished mahogany, "too 'eathen-like."

Only after we had smeared the ball of "Marie's" right thumb with boot-polish and impinged its impression upon the base of the form, would he be satisfied. Then the guardian of the law mounted his bicycle, a little unsteadily, from behind and, with intermittent shakings of the head, had sedately cycled some distance down the road before I realised that I had quite forgotten to ask him to do something about the charabanc parties.

During my absence on the business which I had come home to perform, one minor incident may be worthy of record. That was the occasion on which "Marie" was discovered by my mother whilst engaging herself in the task of giving decent burial to a clutch of eggs in a remote corner of the garden.

"By-n-by plenty velly good," she explained. "Me think after li'l boys b'long big men they velly much likee."

Which reminds me: on the next occasion I visit the Solway Firth, I must remember to have a look and see if they are still there. If so, they should be fairly fruity by this time!

.   .   .   .   .

There is much more that I could recount concerning "Marie": but I will be content to relate, as a final incident, something to set beyond doubt the calibre of woman that she was.

On our return voyage East, as we were approaching the China Sea we were unfortunate enough to strike the full force of a typhoon. I imagine that even to the most hardened sailors in sizable ships, the fury of the typhoon must be a terrifying thing. It certainly was to me, and seemingly so to the handful of others aboard who still remained in a state capable of betraying any emotions at all. For two days and nights, despite battening down and lashing up, one was still conscious of the intermittent thud of heavy objects breaking loose above and below decks and the almost continual crash of crockery from the galleys and pantries. It seemed indeed that all hell had broken loose as the gale howled and screamed relentlessly about us: great seas thundered over the bows as the vessel heeled over so steeply, first to port and then to starboard, that at times one despaired of her ever regaining an even keel.

My wife, a seasoned traveller and normally oblivious to high seas, was completely "out". I could do no more for her than to wedge her into her bunk so that she might avoid being pitched out and flung heavily across the cabin. What "Marie" must have suffered is impossible even to begin endeavouring to imagine: yet no amount of coaxing, bribery, or even the use of harsh words, would persuade her to give up her charges and be left to her agony alone. With pillows and mattresses and everything else soft that she could lay hands on, she had barricaded the boys securely against violent ejection from the bunk where they lay end to end. Clinging to their bed-rail and looking sicker than anyone I have ever seen, she sought to overcome their occasional whimpers and soothe their fears: nothing could defeat that woman.

As the only safe means of locomotion, I crawled back along the corridor on all-fours to our own cabin. Just as I had managed to enter it, the ship broke suddenly from a deep roll to port and, with a cracking wrench of timbers, heaved violently over to starboard: I thought that surely no ship could ride-out such a storm as this and, as the wedges I had placed about my wife fell adrift, I was just able to prevent her prostrate form from being precipitated heavily across the floor. I packed her in again, a little more securely, reassured her concerning "Marie" and the twins and presently crawled back along the corridor to the others.

I found that "Marie" was lying down, now, behind her barricades with a boy securely held within the crook of either arm. Her face was a ghastly colour and seemed distorted with pain as tears, which she had no hand free to check, rolled down her cheeks.

"Marie!" I implored her: but nothing on land or at sea would either shift her or cause her to utter a word of her woes. Clinging on to the bunk opposite, feeling frightened and far from well myself, I watched her at intervals through that night. Despite her intense anguish, she still contrived to hush the children with the whispered measures of *Sha-ke lo tai—Shang-ke lo tai— . . .*

We were clear of the storm by daylight and it was only after I had summoned the harassed and over-worked ship's doctor, I discovered that the violent lurch which so nearly dislodged my wife had taken heavy toll of "Marie". How she crawled back to the twins is a mystery: but how, without giving way and not so much as betraying a hint of what had happened, she was able to withstand the terrible buffeting that followed, is little less than a miracle. Few others on this earth could have managed to do it—at least not with a fractured leg.

But then "Marie" was no ordinary person: and, in common with so many of her country-folk, whom I have been hardly less privileged to know, she had rather a high sense of duty too.

. . . . . .

XI

THE HILL

THE Traveller paused in his climb, looked steadfastly ahead for a moment as though to judge his distance, and then continued on towards the ancient temple which crested the rise and stood guardian over the wide valley that lay beyond.

The old Chinese pedlar, with whom he had conversed the previous day at Tsunwha, had a strange tale to relate concerning this temple that held watch over the Eastern Tombs. But he had heard more, and from many, of the grandeur which it surveyed, and his desire for a brief sharing of such splendour had brought the Traveller a full day's journey under the south shelter of the Great Wall to the halting inn at Malanyu. It was from there, just before sunset, that he had begun to climb the hill.

Now he was at the summit, rather breathlessly crossing the outer precincts of the temple which seemed uncared for and strangely deserted. He passed through the further courtyards and presently into the open again where, beneath a solitary pine, he came to rest. Then, gradually at first, but with increasing significance, an awareness of some new wonder transfixed him as his eyes absorbed the wide panorama that stretched below.

"To look down upon the Eastern Tombs from the hill above Malanyu when the sun is in the far West is among memories immortal," they had told him. Yet to the Traveller such praise seemed strangely insufficient to this setting. The last rays of sun glinting from the Imperial Yellow tiles that adorned a score or more of scattered mausoleums: the dignified magnificence of the tombs themselves which were the ultimate domains of once dragon-throned Emperors: such impressions of material grace were in themselves sufficient for eulogy, but, surpassing the bounds of normal comprehension, there brooded about the scene an atmosphere of spiritual quietude, a profound sense of peace that held the valley immune from the wild wretchedness of the world that lay beyond it.

The years recently passed had borne witness to the new-age armies of the invader marching relentlessly on, had seen five of the great provinces laid waste through modern war: and all China in turmoil. And at this time, not far South of Peking, which lay no more than a hundred *li* to the West, those who had united so that a nation might remain unconquered now grappled together, puppets of opposing political creeds, inspired in passions and equipped with the savagery of weapons all alien to the inherent tranquillity of an age-long elegance.

Down the dusty white highways to the South lurch the rumble and tumble of monster machines and in the cities beyond the plain is the stir and clash and the shriek of arms that bewilder and destroy. The great guns, forged on foreign soil, thunder out to split the skies above some walled and ancient city; a slow half turn on unwieldy mud-caked wheels and they speak again. Then forward, oblivious to the smoke and the rubble and the ruin, heedless of the clamour from the living and the purgatory of the dying. The devilry of modern war persists as a high building falls and a great cloud of dust surges upwards towards the drone of a bombing force fashioned far

153

beyond the borders of its mission. They wheel and scream downwards as the earthbound monsters roll slowly forward by some forgotten arsenal . . . red lightning before one mighty air-rending roar and then annihilation.

But in the valley no flash comes back, no more than a faint echo, born on some idle breeze that but gently stirs the slenderest pine. This is hallowed ground that yet remains sacred for the Lords of the Universe who lie below.

. . . . . .

The Traveller tried hard to define the element that held him there, entranced beyond the more earthly considerations of mere spectacle or modern sentiment for a splendour that could be no more. It was perhaps the mystery of the unknown, he thought; for down there among the Immortals of their time lay the secrets of forgotten dynasties. There, rested the bones of Emperors who sprang from a civilisation older than any that is known. Their lives were deep-rooted in beliefs that were born before history and their faith in the hereafter was sublime. So it was until, with the pomp and ceremony that was their due, they came to the plain below, on their last journey East from Peking. And as they passed further, unescorted, beyond the provinces that are known, the pattern of their lives might pass as good token when they reached *The Yellow Springs*.

The wide mountain range to the North grew dusky in the half light and the shadow of the hill was lengthening along the way that led to the East. Above it and beyond, winding interminably through the darkening distance, still sentinel above the furthest peak, stretched the jagged unbroken line that was the Great Wall of China.

The Watcher by the temple remained immovable, as though he had become absorbed into the drowsy still peace that reigned above the sleeping kings. High beauty was in the air and a tranquility which his age had never known, enveloped him.

He rested there unaccompanied but strangely not alone while that ace of Tricksters—Time—slipped back through four decades.

.   .   .   .   .   .

Now he knew that a presence was beside him; a being intangible that spoke with the soft accents of the Manchu dialect. The gentle voice came to him as a whispered echo.

"Look your way to the West, Foreign Friend; faint sounds will follow the dawn and then draw nearer, as slowly the pageant that was Peking unfolds from the dust to pass majestically on its ultimate errand." The voice paused, then added in more pronounced tones, "Look well, for this is the very end of an era."

Shortly, borne on a light breeze came the single note of a funeral horn and a fluff of white dust rose across the distant edge of the plain. It seemed as though the cloud moved slowly towards the hill, bearing in its approach the deep intermittent clang of a gong and the high clash of cymbals that echoed back across the valley from the Northern heights. Soon, nearer came the wail of lamentation rising and falling above the sing-song chant of a hundred and twenty bearers. Then slowly emerging into view came their burden: the huge catafalque appearing as some great gaudily-arrayed marquee and the plain became suddenly alive with colour and movement and the eerie noises that are of half-unleashed emotion. At the head of this glittering cortège marched a bodyguard of Manchu princes and all the members of the Grand Council, whose habit it had been to meet their ruler at the dawn of each day in the Hall of Perfect Harmony.

A question had hardly framed itself on the Traveller's lips before the answer came softly from beside him.

"Tz'u Hsi, Empress Dowager and last of the Celestial ones; she ruled China for five decades and died in the ninth year of your present century."

Behind the mighty catafalque rode mounted troops followed by the slow ambling gait of camels accompanied by their Mongol attendants. Then borne aloft in procession came a kaleidoscope of the gay honorific umbrellas that had welcomed Her Majesty back from exile eight years earlier. In contrast followed a sedate file of high Lama dignitaries in their sombre robes, then a host of white-clad officials bearing Manchu sacrificial vessels of carved jade, massive incense bearers of gold and silver, Buddhist symbols and colourfully-embroidered panels. Slowly the long cortège moved up and halted at the end of its four-day journey from The Forbidden City. Three splendid chariots with trappings and curtains of Imperial Yellow silk, emblazoned with dragon and phoenix and two state palanquins similarly arrayed, passed on their majestic way and then came to rest. And now the great conclave were about the mausoleum, the most magnificent of them all, built by the faithful Jung Lu for his Imperial mistress at a cost calculated at eight million of Taels. The dust drifted upwards and dispersed as the end of the long procession drew up and the final ceremony at the tomb began.

The richly-jewelled couch was ready to receive the coffin

while about it were assembled the carved figures of serving maids and eunuchs, destined, it seemed, to stand for ever in attendance. The Princes, Chamberlains and high officials of the Manchu dynasty made ready to take their final farewell of the illustrious dead, while the succeeding Empress Dowager, and the surviving consorts of the Imperial house, offered the last rites in the mortuary chamber.

From the Hill it was as though the Traveller was existing through some as yet unexplored dimension: that he sensed more than saw a ritual that was forty years old being re-enacted on the plain below. The conviction, too, became borne upon him that the quiet voice at his side was ageless and the whispering echo of some far richer decade. Indeed it seemed that he stood within a magic circle which was immune from the standards that set a yesterday and a tomorrow. His being had become merged in the unchanging and dateless philosophy where forty years are but a moment and death is no more than a gentle closing of the eyes and a tranquil journeying on.

Again he was aware of the soft tones of the Manchu dialect that somehow divined and then provided expression to his train of thought.

"The two great doors of stone descend for the resting place of the Empress Tz'u Hsi to be closed for ever. Alas! that it might have been so. It should be that at the instant of that closing, the spirit of the departed ruler is translated to Her Majesty's Ancestral Tablet. It is in itself no more than a simple strip of carved and lacquered wood, but it is accorded honour and ceremony equal with that which was credited to the sovereign during her lifetime. You see the gorgeous chariot draped with yellow silk that bears its light burden aloft, back

157

from the plain to Peking, along the Imperial way that is swept hourly by a thousand men. There, with ceremony unsurpassed in any age or era, the Tablet is accorded its rightful place in the Temple of Ancestors that lies behind the high walls of the Forbidden City. So the spirit returns, perchance to find rest awhile, until the call comes for the ceremony at the Yellow Springs where body and soul are cleansed anew and reunited to roam at will among the sunlit hills of Enduring Concord."

The soft tones melted away, and a sudden darkness descended over the whole valley. Thunder pealed out above the high hills to the North which echoed and reverberated across the wide plain, while angry stabs of lightning seemed to pierce down into the very earth itself.

"Time," the voice whispered above the storm, "Time still plays philanderer. To the mind that would use it for measure you are moving forward instantly through two decades. Now watch as the lightning strikes . . ."

Then the Traveller saw that from a pageant of reverential splendour the scene at the tomb of the Great Empress had transformed itself into one of stark horror. A rabble of shouting grey-clad figures had torn asunder the great doors of the mausoleum and were rifling the mortuary chamber of its precious contents, the trappings of a Queen that were for her accompaniment through the gardens of fragrance. Loaded and then borne away on crude oxen carts were the sacrificial vessels, the incense burners of gold and silver and the carved jade and ivory figures that had stood watch over their Imperial Mistress for just under twenty years. Nothing seemed sacred to this unaccountable mob of sacrilegious vandals—nothing. A blinding flash from the skies revealed the most unbelievable

horror of all—*the body was being dragged out from the coffin* . . .
It was something most shockingly macabre, so grotesquely
unreal as to be indefinable. Yet the Traveller knew that it had
actually happened. It was done, he recollected, by the disbanded, unpaid soldiers of an avenging war-lord; some said at
the instigation of an uncouth and callous authority. That was
immaterial; the tragedy lay in the poignant fact that it happened.

As swiftly as it had descended, the storm passed and a blazing
sun bore down on the plain betraying the now deserted and
empty tomb. Near at hand lay the naked body of the Great
Dowager Empress with every feature still perfectly intact, and
even in such utter abandonment strangely calm and serene.
And she lay there exposed, yet quite impervious, to the
changing elements of numberless days.

Then, unaccountably, she was there no longer as the voice,
still gently, yet a little more urgently, breathed again at his side.

"It is no more than the symbol of a restless age. The deep
sorrows of China are closely interwoven with those of Tz'u
Hsi: voyagers in suspense, since mortals do not choose to leave
them undisturbed. For centuries the Empire that was China was
changeless and immune: the dawn of her civilisation is dateless,
though for a thousand years it has gradually declined. But the
ancient Sages were wise in their time and their elegant philo-
sophies, steeped in the old laws of cultural perfection, have
lived on down the dynasties. They will continue to exist
through the period of adjustment while the best, for a while,
must needs lie dormant. The factor of Time is immaterial; for
Progress—no scribe has designed a character to portray its
meaning. Prosperity is known; it is born and lives solely within

the mind at rest. No culture, no art, in their unchanging fashions were practised elsewhere in higher degree: no change can ever destroy such refinements, for China is essentially unchangeable. Four hundred millions of her people have been content to crave no more than a meagre life from the soil about their homes and the divine right to indulge the sacred code of filial piety. The great continent, once proudly ruled from the Dragon-throne, is stirring restlessly, but the influences that despoil her were beyond her wide horizons. The Invaders have come—the Mongols and the Tartars and the little men from the islands to the East. The outer provinces have been dispossessed for such that you term as time; it is nothing more than transitory, for always the people will return and the country remain mistress of her own destinies. China is vast, she is all absorbing; tolerant of her transgressors, unchanging in the relentless march of events about her; inscrutable, immovable and quite unconquerable. It is appropriate for it to be known that the country which the Great Emperors once ruled must suffer the internal strife of readjustment; that it is a phase in the struggle to recapture a spirit of Nationalism which was lost when twilight fell over the Forbidden City. The surge is so that an ordered unity may replace the days of chaos and yield the nation strength from which will be born anew the old independence. There are the expediencies of the East, used in some measure to counter those of the West, but there is no ideology that does not spring naturally from the hearts and minds of the people. China will never become heir to a doctrine that tends to destroy her heritage of human rights nor will she bear the yoke of overlords from beyond her borders. She is ever intolerant of influences that would defile the elegance of her ancient culture, and men should know the uselessness of their endeavours to implant upon her the ways that are not written in her philosophy. In the history of China forty years are no more than a moment and immune from the ruins that your Progress brings about the world, hereabouts may once more become the cradle of a calmer civilisation. It is no more than a matter of values."

There was a pause and when the voice spoke again it was no more than just the breath of a whisper.

"Foreign Friend, you have come to The Hill, as no doubt others may, in search of something. You will have found only this: that in the great heart of countless millions of Chinese people there is dignity, pride and sufficiency. Their desire in life is as simple as was Tz'u Hsi's in death—*to be left undisturbed*. Now rest for a while before you travel on beyond The Hill in your full world with its yesterdays and its to-morrows. As you go, may you yet remember and repeat and respect that simple phrase: it is the message of Malanyu."

". . . to be left undisturbed."

A chill breeze stirred the branches of the pine trees under which he lay. Gradually the Traveller became aware of a strange emptiness that was in the atmosphere about him—an uneasy sense of being suddenly alone. A wandering mist swept clear of The Hill and a pale moon was shining across the valley where the Great Emperors lay at rest.

· · · · · · ·

XII

PORTRAIT OF A WAR LORD

MENG LI FU was not his real name; neither for that matter was the one by which he was universally known. In China there is much in a name: that which may be inherited from less exacting or ambitious forebears is liable, if inappropriate, to prove a handicap to those who seek the highest ascendancy in their particular choice of profession. Whereas, I think it may be said, there is nothing in these Islands to prevent an Englishman who may be called Smelling-Fowler from becoming an Archbishop or an Admiral of the Fleet, there exists in China a far greater tendency for a man's name to be regarded as a clue to his characteristics. Consequently a Chinese with the inherited appellation of "Swaying Bamboo"—suggesting that he be no more than a reed shaken by the wind—would enjoy but little chance of ever becoming a War Lord unless he took steps to exchange it for one that was more appropriate. Marshal Meng, who was nothing if not astute, had, quite early in his military career, rectified precisely such a state of affairs, thus enabling him subsequently to emerge into official prominence as "Lord of the Elegant Sword".

Less officially, in the course of his swashbuckling rise to Military Governorship, he had, in addition, acquired one or two other titles. His soldiers, who spontaneously regarded him as Deity, referred to him in open reverence as "Tiger Fang"; but the provincial peasantry, whom he taxed well-nigh out of existence, dubbed him (though always from a safe distance) "The Monster Leech of Loyang". In strange and simple contrast, I addressed him, though but once and at his request, as "Herbert": a title too incongruous by far, when I came to think of it, for a young foreigner habitually to bestow upon an ageing quite heathen Marshal of Chinese Armies who held, and indeed exercised, the power of life and death over tens of millions of people. Besides, though it might be while the Kaoliang wine flowed freely he liked me to consider him the Kitchener of China and address him familiarly as such, he was subject to such quick and quite unaccountable changes of mood that an ill-timed "Herbert" might have served to sever our relations, if indeed not improbably, my head.

At heart, though by no means in mind, Marshal Meng was essentially a simple man; but perceived through Occidental eyes, certain of his habits and practices might well give rise to doubts concerning his over-all merit. But, for my part, maintaining that it was quite inappropriate for two adherents to well-accepted, yet widely different, ways of life to condemn the ideas and actions of the other, I never considered it my business to judge him. Neither is this rough sketch of a remarkable and often astonishing man, who projected his personality so forcibly upon my Western mind, designed in criticism or as a caricature: it is no more than an unvarnished portrait drawn from still vivid memories of an all too brief encounter.

.   .   .   .   .   .

It took me nearly two weeks to discover that in the course of my vain endeavours to meet Marshal Meng, I had succeeded in

163

becoming no more than a source of unearned income to a host of those appointed to be responsible for his protection. On first boldly advancing to the outer gates of his palatial *Yamen* I was immediately arrested by a scruffy-looking sentry equipped with Sherlock Holmes' hat, bulging bandolier, a carbine to which was attached by wire an instrument like a meat-skewer and, as a touch of the more modern Mars, two Mills bombs hung with twine which dangled precariously from his belt hooks. It cost me a dollar to speak to the sergeant and two more to interview the Lieutenant who, in exchange for my cigarettes, suggested I should return on the morrow. On that and subsequent days I persevered with the costly expedient of allowing myself to be initially arrested, released and, at ever-increasing expense, passed through successive ranks to be dismissed on each occasion at the level of one grade higher. I suffered this daily experience thus far in the knowledge that it was in accordance with accepted procedure; and on the eleventh day perseverance was rewarded by my introduction to an unshaven character, with cotton wool bursting forth from his quilted tunic, who purported to be a General. He, having intimated (not without avail) that he was temporarily embarrassed to the extent of twenty-five dollars, presently proceeded to inform me, with an elegant display of courteous apology, that the *Tuchan* was absent on a visit to his native Loyang. It was then I decided that this extravagant form of tom-foolery was obviously no more than wasted effort; no one among my inquisitors had even enquired as to what might be the nature of my business with the Marshal; and when, on one occasion, I volunteered the information, it was met by a conspicuous lack of interest. So, accompanied only by a sense of frustration and the little that was left of my "ready", I turned my steps somewhat disconsolately away—back in the direction of the Treaty port from whence I had speculatively come.

But I had not travelled so much as a *li* from the *Yamen* gates before I heard the unmistakable clatter of many horsemen ahead and observed a cloud of dust rolling towards me from the distance. I stepped hurriedly off the narrow and crudely-metalled track out of the way of their swift approach; and presently what appeared to be a heavily-armed squadron of Chinese cavalry came cantering into view. The detachment, about thirty strong, was preceded by a pair of out-riders bearing heavy executioner's swords over their shoulders, the main body riding four abreast immediately behind a standard bearer. They were uniformly clad in light grey padded coats topped by rather moth-eaten looking fur caps with ear flaps; each had a bandolier and a carbine slung across his shoulder and bumped along uneasily astride sturdy, though ill-groomed, Mongolian ponies. But in the very centre of the cavalcade, flanked by another pair of ceremonial swordsmen, rode an outstanding and quite exceptional figure: he was far more smartly accoutred than the rest and, in even greater contrast, was reining in a magnificent beast which from every appearance might well have been foaled on The Curragh. By every precept this figure should have been the fabulous Marshal himself; obviously, though, he was not; since the centrepiece around which this grizzly escort moved was beyond all doubt a Foreigner: moreover, I observed to my amazement, as in passing he cast a critical glance at me standing ankle-deep in a paddy, that the features were more than familiar: they were unmistakably those of the ever-adventurous "Mad-boy" McCammond who had caused Treaty-port life to become both the quieter and the poorer by his disappearance from its then gay security some six or so years earlier. I was in two minds as to whether or not I should turn back: I was sufficiently intrigued to try and learn more and besides, there at least was a man who might well prove the means of subsequently assisting my mission. But on further reflection I came to the conclusion that even to see "Mad-boy" again and listen to his story—no doubt a fascinating one—was not worth the risk of a new series of expensive arrests. Then, almost immediately after I had started again on my way, I was aware of galloping hooves behind me and in turning I saw, like a flash, the familiar figure as though all in one effortless action draw level, rein in and dismount:

"It's yourself sure enough, then," he greeted me.

" 'Mad-boy', this is grand!" I cried. "So you did recognise me?"

"Sure, and how could I not." Then suddenly, looking slightly apprehensive, he added, "And how the divil did you know I was here?"

I could hardly restrain a smile. Whatever he was up to, "Mad-boy" had apparently lost none of his Irish conceit.

"If I'd known *you* were here," I replied, "I probably wouldn't have been arrested on eleven successive days on charges of attempting to see the Marshal."

He threw back his head and laughed. "Praise be to the pigs!" he exclaimed. " 'Tis always the same. But come along now and if it's himself that you're after, then sure 'tis aisy enough for you to be seeing him to-day."

We started back, I with mingled feelings of surprise and delight.

"But tell me," I asked, "what in the name of all that's insane have you got yourself up to now?"

"Praise be! And did you not know I'm a General," he replied, "and indeed I'm prouder still of the tidy price that's set about my head; it's a long story I'd be telling. But now what will it be that brings you after plaguing the Marshal?"

"Well!" I exclaimed, thankful that somebody had actually asked me at last. "It's roads: I believe there's a big scheme afoot for threading the Province with roads. I'm only interested commercially," I added with caution.

What I gathered to be two bodyguards had now joined us and taken over my companion's horse as we slowly retraced our way to the *Yamen.*

"Roads," he reflected. "Yes and indeed there was a scheme but now . . . anyhow, you'll be talking to the Marshal; it's himself that better be telling you."

"I've just paid twenty-five dollars for the privilege of learning that 'Himself' is in Loyang," I informed him.

"And indeed he was: what would you be thinking the dust storm you were gazing at from the paddy just now was all about? Sure it was no more than 'Himself' coming back from Loyang."

"The Marshal!" I exclaimed. "Marshal Meng—but . . . but which was he?"

"You may ask," came the reply, "for I'm never quite certain myself: you see he'll always be riding as one of the escort."

"Indeed! Is that caution or democracy?" I enquired.

"Divil, and it's a bit of 'em both," replied 'Mad-boy', "but he does it, I'd be saying, chiefly for the fun of the thing."

I smiled. "He must be a character."

"A character you're saying! He's a barrel-full of monkeys in mischief and cruder by far than McGhinty's back-yard: but he's as fine a man as ever you'll be meeting. I'd die for him every day, even if 'twere not my job to be doing just that."

I was about to ask my friend the extent to which he was rewarded for this quaintly-expressed privilege when there was a metallic clatter on the stone cobbles just as we regained the outer approaches to the *Yamen*. I observed that my now-startled acquaintance, the scruffy sentry so much of whose daily routine had been lately taken up in arresting me, was in the act of presenting arms: it was a remarkable performance made even more distinctive by the fact that in its process the meat-skewer became detached from the muzzle of his carbine and, as we passed, lay adjacent to a pair of carpet-slippered ex-tremities.

"You'll be welcome in my quarters," my friend was saying, "they're roomy enough and Danny—the pilot—'s away."

I murmured my thanks.

"Sure and you can stay," he went on, "if indeed for the love of Michael you'll not be crying out your eyes with laughing, or be forfeiting your head for the loss of his Face."

I began deliberating with some apprehension on the extent to which acceptance might prejudice my fond hopes for a long future.

"Of course," I said, rather lamely, "it's very good of you . . . very good indeed of you . . . I . . ."

"Not at all, at all, now," he interrupted me, "I'll arrange for

168

the Marshal to be seeing you at six. 'Tis the hour before that is
his sacred one."

"Sacred one?" I enquired. "The hour of Mogreb or something?"

'Mad-boy' was smiling. " 'Himself'," he said, "is, if you'll
not be knowing it, a High Priest among Heathen. I might be
telling you about that hour; but 'tis better, maybe, yourself
should be finding out; and if you'll be curbing that gape of
surprise, he'll be showing you the finest man to be born beyond
Kerry—and a bag-full of pranks besides."

. . . . . .

I was indeed surprised, if not bewildered, from the first
moment of my meeting with the Marshal. I thought 'Mad-boy'
must have been back at his old tricks when he ushered me into
an apartment which was utterly devoid of any furniture or
adornments save for a single bench set against one of the bare
and crudely-plastered walls. In the middle of this rickety form
sat a huddled and begrimed creature clothed in such tattered
garments to appear as though he were some impoverished
outlaw. I glanced over my shoulder and noted that the door had
been closed behind me so that I stood alone in a state of embarrassed uncertainty before this strange and sorry figure who
neither looked up nor made manifest the slightest stir of life at
my entrance. Then it dawned on me that this must be an ante-
room to the Marshal's private apartment and that if I instilled
into the bedraggled creature before me the urgency of my
appointment, something would assuredly happen. I tried it,
only to find that my idea was a mistaken one, which caused me

169

a quite natural degree of irritation. Raising my voice to some semblance of authority, I enquired in Chinese who he was, adding that it would be as well that he answer my question, if indeed he was equipped with the faculties of hearing and speech. That utterance caused him to stir, though no more than perceptibly. But the reply which it evoked, surprising in itself, staggered me the more through the fact that it was not framed in the local dialect but delivered in the soft measured tones of Mandarin.

"I can hear and I can speak. You ask me who I am. I answer I am a common servant. You are, I suppose, an Englishman, for you are impatient and obviously lacking a little in elegance. What might it be that you want?"

Intrigued though I was, I recovered my composure quickly, since I found myself to be little enamoured by the twist of this clever ruffian's tongue.

"I have an appointment with the Marshal," I replied brusquely. "Please show me to him immediately."

The tattered and uncouth creature before me then slowly raised his head and looked at me straight in the eyes. As he did so, I vividly remember being immediately in mind of some children's pantomime where the grotesque and ugly ogre is, in a flash, transformed into a glittering figure of princeliness. An exaggerated metaphor maybe, but it is true to say that the man's countenance held so much for me, it was as though the tattered trappings and generally begrimed appearance had all magically fallen away, creating the obvious impression that they were in effect no more than some motley. A countenance so rich in infinite wisdom and so full of fearless intent, it was in every way the most striking among any I have so far seen: it was indeed

a remarkable face. Within its expression lay also the unmistakable mark of the ruthless; but, piercing those half-hooded
sinister shadows, shone a light which I discerned to be kindly:
and I found it precious to behold in that moment, when I became aware that the features which I held in my focus were
indisputably those of the Marshal.

Clumsily, of course, I endeavoured to make amends in the
performance of a salutation which, in its confused uneasiness of
East and West, became a blundering fool no better. I clicked
my heels, then bobbed my head three times towards him:
said, "Your Excellency" in Chinese and added "Sorry," in
my own tongue: in all, I suppose, a pretty poor pattern of
apology.

"*Mai yeo fa'tze,*" he said, rather wearily I thought: and then,
as though it might be in mimicry, astounded me by interpreting
the expression into English. "It is," he repeated, "of little
account."

Then, with an elegant gesture, he removed his hands from
within the frayed folds of their opposite sleeves and motioned
me to be seated beside him. I could not help but observe those
hands: to his general unkempt and bedraggled appearance, they
were as much in contrast as was the form of his face and expression: they were most exquisitely shaped and, beneath the
grime, undoubtedly smooth. Somehow it was difficult to escape
a conviction that the dirt had been deliberately applied; it was
as though the man were a well-bred actor cast in the rôle of
destitute beggar. And here I was to find that, for once, my
conviction was perfectly right.

Obeying his injunction, I composed myself at his side with a
considerable degree of caution; for the bench we now shared

was crudely enough carpentered so as to sway perilously beneath us upon a pair of ill-attached rests. Thus I sat for a time, in mortal dread, not daring to imagine such a scene as might ensue should this frailty fail to uphold the full course of our exchanges. Already I had been embarrassed enough and prayed only to be spared the weight of final catastrophe.

"To-morrow," said the Marshal, reverting suddenly to his native tongue, "I beg that you will honour me by acceptance of my hospitality in an atmosphere more appropriate to a foreign guest of obvious distinction. To-day, I would crave your pardon and ask you to excuse me: I am weary and not a little troubled."

I thanked him; and in emphasis of my appreciation and sympathy inclined myself gracefully from the waist towards him: hastily, however, I made frantic endeavour to restore equilibrium and with but a fraction of time to spare: for, as though to mock my movement, the seat had inclined in equal degree to the accompaniment of an ominous creak, causing the Marshal, who must needs be borne with it, a moment of alert apprehension. That put "paid" to any attempts at elegance: I was much too precariously perched for further excursions into the courtesies of China. Henceforward I posed in the sadly-lost style once assumed by cockaded footmen of Edwardian England whose immobile attitude above the box bestowed dignity upon the crested carriages of Society in days that were more spacious.

"To-morrow," continued the War-lord, as calm became fully restored, "you will feast with the Marshal Meng Li Fu. Just now, you honour with your company no more than his most humble servant; a fact," he concluded, "which, to judge from your manner was obviously apparent on your entry."

"No one," I protested in all sincerity, "could fail to detect the Lord of the Elegant Sword; even though he may, for good reasons unknown to me, adopt the trappings that would better become the bandit."

As I finished my sentence I became conscious of the fact that he was for the first time regarding me with an obvious degree of interest.

"You speak my language surprisingly well for a foreigner," he remarked, "and the turn of your phrase suggests that you were born to be wise. But I fear I must call you to a state of correction. These trappings, as you term them, are those of Lao Er, the lowest of all my menials and who, as you earlier suggested, is normally mute. But, as yet, not *one* among the force which form the *Yamen* guard, nor indeed within the garrisons beyond, has proclaimed me, thus guised, as Lord of the Elegant Sword."

"But surely—your features . . ." I began.

With no more than an elegant twist of his hand, he bade me hold my words; and then proceeded on:

"You must be unaware, I think, of certain matters: the first concerns me, the rest are affairs among the men of my armies. Was I not born to become a Marshal of China, then indeed I should have been known as an actor—less talented, maybe, than Mei Lang Fan—but certainly more robust."

He paused as though to allow the significance of this statement its due measure of appreciation; and then continued:

"It is perhaps well I be so endowed with the ability to play a part. You see; there is much that may be said in the presence of

173

one who is widely believed to lack the gifts of hearing and speech. Thus it is that the mute menial, by whom you sit, may sweep at will about the quarters of the Guard or, at such times as his uncertain health permit, boil tea for those who argue in idleness about the barrack-room. Lao Er, you will understand, must needs be a sickly man equipped with an absentee warrant which applies whenever the Marshal has affairs elsewhere. In effect, though, by some strange unquestioned artifice that is all his own, the same sick servant contrives to follow the High Tuchan on his many missions to the Garrisons further afield; and if, perchance, the Marshal must unwillingly treat with the scum of a so-called Central Government, the slatternly presence of his silent shadow performs an essentially significant service."

The War-lord cleared his throat as though to indicate that his utterances were still short of their climax.

"I am told," he went on, "that you are an Englishman with a high sense of honour; and therefore I have no doubt that, in accordance with your Western Code, I may belittle myself in your mind by the fact that I spy upon my soldiers. It is a pity if this be so, since it is my desire that, in exchange for my confidences, you, in turn, may [honour me with certain of yours."

He continued immediately, as though to safeguard his remarks against the slightest intrusion: "So first I must explain this poor wretch (who has been tortured and horse-whipped and was once all but hanged by disorderly elements among my Guard), and tell you why I cannot as yet, grant him his only wish, which is the privilege of peacefully dying. As it is, I may well die first, since these days are precarious and the elements of

174

treachery abound in whichever direction I may turn the deaf ears of Lao Er. I must know the extent of it and from whence it springs; there is much that I have learnt in the past few days; but . . ." he stopped abruptly. "Why do you look at me in such surprise?"

"I . . . I must beg your pardon," I stammered, "I thought . . ."

"Of course," he reassured me. "The Marshal was indeed in Loyang; but Lao Er has not been blind to the discomforts of your several arrests. You are a persistent man, I think: perhaps you will inform me of the cost of your persistence in the matter of bribes."

"It is of no account," I replied briefly.

"Then I, too, can be persistent," said the Marshal severely, "I would like to know how much you paid to the officers and men of the *Yamen* Guard."

"Well—" I made a rapid calculation and divided the answer by half, "certainly not more than forty-five dollars in all."

"*Ai Ya!*" exclaimed the War-lord. "You have paid my soldiers forty-five dollars!"

"Perhaps it was not quite so much," I added rather nervously.

"If you paid them ninety dollars," replied the Marshal, "I should have been better pleased; because you see," he blandly concluded, "now for six moons past I have paid them nothing at all."

I was struck by the frankness of his utterance which explained so much that I had recently experienced and seen.

"Forty-five dollars," he reflected, "adds an urgency to your persistence: and is it, as the Irish General suggests, all in aid of my roads?"

"Not in their construction, "I explained, seizing this unexpected opportunity to expand upon the objects of my mission, "but there is a substance which hardens the surface. It . . ."

"We will forbear for the moment," he broke in, "to discuss any questions of surface: there are matters which to me are of much deeper moment. I have the wish to know, first, the Englishman's impression of *me*."

This was wholly unexpected.

"I have no knowledge of official opinion," I replied tactfully, "since I am neither of the Embassy nor of the Consular service. But whole-heartedly I will proclaim my own, which is widely shared, and say you are regarded as a soldier of brave distinction, an administrator of considerable merit and, over-all, a figure never-failing in its ability to capture the imagination of the multitude. Politically, it is a matter of common knowledge that you are out of sympathy with the Central Government and that in no greater degree are you attracted to their perpetual enemies—the new People's Army—whose rising strength Nanking but vainly endeavours to suppress. It is thought," I continued, "at least by the Traders, that you may well be such a man as might hold the balance of power between these main elements of continual civil strife, since on whichever side you might choose to throw the weight of your loyal and independent armies should serve in itself to settle the issue."

The suggestion of a sigh escaped the Marshal: "I would surrender Life that it might be so," he whispered. And then on a louder, more hopeful note he added, "As it is, it must, I suppose, be the roads: indeed there may be only the roads left on which to depend for the continued existence of my power and the maintenance of all my men at arms. So *unless*,"—he laid em-

phasis on the word—"unless it may happen that you and your
Trader friends will lend some measure of practical support to
the polite opinions you have so elegantly expressed, then, as a
last resort I must turn to the highways to deaden the attention
of my troops to the rebellious elements; the infiltrators who are
finding their way into each of all the scattered Garrisons that
house, what you have generously termed, my loyal and independent armies. A soldier, you know," he continued more
slowly and softly, "is first of all human: he remains loyal and
independent for only so long: after a time it is natural that his
independence must needs be fortified by some token for his
service, lest his loyalty become liable to barter among Agents
from the armies of others."

While he paused for a moment I endeavoured to sort out in
my mind the significance of what he had said. But I completely
failed to fathom how it might be that the construction of highways would serve to prevent the desertion of unpaid troops to
forces which were opposed to his. As to his alternative suggestion, I had no doubt that it was his intention to become
more precise.

"If, as you suggest," the War-lord went on presently, "that
I hold the balance of power in China, is that not in itself a
sufficiency upon which to come to agreement? I am aware of
the millions of British money tied up in the Treaty ports and
which, in the passage of time, I would warn you, may well
become forfeit. Now; were I to offer, for development, to
your Industrialists and Engineers, the wide virgin territories of
China that are beholden to me—in themselves both vaster and
richer in wealth than all England—would you not, in return for
such monopoly, extend your support and indulgence to me?"

M   177

This astounding offer, which I took as being genuine, led me to take refuge from immediate commitment behind long-winded explanations concerning Government recognitions, International agreements and Commercial treaties about which, I may say, my knowledge was probably on a par with that of the sentry in the Sherlock Holmes' hat.

He lent polite ear to this rambling discourse until such time as I dried up completely; then he replied with a patient air:

"But I think you misunderstand me. I am well aware that this is a matter which cannot be negotiated through the Diplomatic Authorities whose letters of credence are addressed to the Central Government. For this reason it is to *you*—please understand to you personally—that I am making this offer; since I am told that you are the representative of perhaps the most prominent among all British industries possessing wide interests which are quite independent of Governments and Embassies. To you, alone, therefore, I am affording the opportunity of a great development in your own interests; in return for which I would ask no more than—shall we say—a few hundred thousand of taels in first token of good faith and understanding. I think it is a bargain which you would be wise to accept."

It seemed hard to grasp the fact that I had come here in the hope of selling an experimental ton or two of surface hardening, only to find myself sharing a precarious bench with a fabulous War-lord, dressed up as a deaf and dumb coolie, who was seriously trying to interest me in the purchase of eighty thousand square miles of Central China.

"Will you accept ? " he insisted.

178

"But, Marshal," I pleaded, "this cannot be decided by me."

"It cannot!" he shouted in tones of rising anger. "It cannot! Then who are you who dares to intrude upon my time. Must I remind you that I am Meng Li Fu—a Marshal of China, the dignity of whose position confines his attentions solely to others who are of sufficient eminence to provide his proposals with an instant 'Yes' or 'No' ? "

This riled me: the man was being childish. "Very well, your Excellency," I said coldly, "then I will give you an immediate reply: the answer is 'No'."

I sat stock still in the deathly hush that ensued which was eventually broken by the War-lord's reversion to a manner more normal.

"You are a brave man," he said quietly, "and I respect you the more for it." He paused and then added more slowly, "Tell me—at what would you assess your worth ? "

"My worth ? "

"Shall we say—ten thousand taels ? "

"You mean . . ."

"You suggested," he explained, "that my trappings might better become the bandit: maybe I might better become the character too: since, unless my roads mature with promptitude, I will indeed be a desperate man. It would be easy—very easy, I think—to hold you to hostage, though—of course—an honoured guest, for as many weeks as it might take your Industrial Lords to negotiate terms for your release. Do you not agree ? "

Having delivered himself of this ominous statement, he regarded me with intent for a second before becoming suddenly charged with a new sense of urgency. As it were all in one instant he shuffled his feet, rose abruptly and moved swiftly to the door which I was presently aware had closed behind him. It was a manoeuvre, which in that moment of my grave apprehension, could not have been more perfectly timed to catch me off guard. As I picked myself up a little painfully from the floor, I could not but believe that it was deliberately done. I stood dusting my suit, rather stupidly surveying the splintered remains of the bench with a folded-up end and vaguely speculated on what there might be to follow. Then the door fell slightly ajar again and "Mad Boy's" head appeared, as it might be a conspirator's, round it.

"Praise be to the Almighty!" he whispered, "surely now and you've not been allowing him to upset yourself?"

"Oh no!" I replied in louder tones. "But, if you have such a thing in captivity, I could surely use a drink."

. . . .

"Eight swords!" I ventured, thrusting forward three fingers of my right hand; but the wily Marshal had simultaneously shot out no more than an elegant two. In strict unison we closed our respective palms to throw them open again with a changed display of digits and his accompanying call of "Five Bamboos!" The estimate was no more correct; so the traditional contest continued until the loser was found and called to pay forfeit: the result, I felt sure, was a foregone conclusion, since the War-lord in his cups was craftier still.

"Nine Stars!" he bellowed.

"Four flowers!" I countered.

"One Phoenix."

"Six scrolls—ah!" His fully open palm mocked at my solitary upraised finger while the Marshal graciously bowed to me as a victor may to the vanquished. I, in turn, appropriately raised my cup, brim-full of the warm wine from kaoliang, first to him with a ringing "*kam-bei*" and then to my lips; for the measure, in accordance with tradition, to be drained in a single quaff.

"*Ai Ya!*" exclaimed the War-lord. "What the Irish General has told me is right. It seems, indeed, that both your legs must be hollow."

As I put my cup down it was immediately replenished from a burnished kettle by an exquisite maiden from whose raven, tightly-bound hair a camellia blossomed: and whose form was so elegantly slender as to be scarcely discernible beneath a gown of patterned brocade fashioned high to the throat and slit—*à la mode*—from ankle to knee.

In answer to my formal enquiries she proclaimed herself to be "White Floating Lotus" and seventeen in the first moon of the coming year. She was certainly wise to the use of cosmetics: and I should hazard, behind a coy façade, to the ways of the world as well.

"White Floating Lotus" was utterly mine. With an extravagant gesture, accompanied by a full recital of Chinese histrionics, Marshal Meng Li Fu had, half-way through the fourteenth dish, made me an entirely unsolicited gift of her. For himself, despite an outward air of utter indifference, he appeared well content with the yet younger charms of "Precious Blue Hill". Her close and quite immovable proximity to the Marshal's chair proclaimed her a hussy, while it afforded the War-lord but the use of one overworked hand for attention to the abundant claims of his chop-sticks, his cup, his more elegant gestures and an increasing insistance to engage me in the finger-game.

"W. F. Lotus" and "P. B. Hill" as the droll pilot "Danny" proclaimed them, had just arrived at the *Yamen* by air from Shanghai. It was all in the day's work for "Danny" to purchase such playthings for the Marshal; but, as the pilot put it to me, "the Old Man's apt to be choosey and 'tain't no picnic neither, when I'm ordered to return 'The Empties'."

Apart from the playthings, we were a party of five (until "Danny" passed quietly out) and the night was designed on a truly Imperial scale. Certainly the Marshal was *en fête* and, in his gala rig, a striking contrast to the equally unforgettable figure who had so unceremoniously unsettled me on the evening before. Now he was resplendent in a uniform (fashioned, I was told, from his own design) of blue and scarlet and gold, emblazoned by unpurposeful trappings and an extravagant cluster of orders in odd design. Were it not for the *Gendarme's* hat (two sizes too small with a "bobble" on top), which reposed upon his head throughout the night, there was an affinity about his attire with that which I once saw worn by a French Fire-chief at a function in the town of Tours. But whether thus fabulously arrayed, or garbed in extreme disrepute, it was of little account to one such as I so drawn by the strange magnetism of the Marshal's mien: be it indeed as before, unshaven and deliberately begrimed, or as now, with its smooth features flushed with wine and lit by the glow of abandon, it was ever a face indescribably brave; and, in moments of unguarded repose, still charged with the wisdom of all things, set off by an air of effortless grace. I found it utterly impossible to believe that even the dullest among his near-million garrisoned men could fail for a moment to detect that the eyes of a mute Lao Er were in reality those of the Marshal. This led me to wonder how much I should accept among the things which he had said on the previous day. Could this brave face have been carved on a figure of no more than fabulous fun, or was it just that he was a man possessed of a puckish wit? Was he certain that I would sprawl on the floor when he suddenly rose from the rickety bench and, of paramount importance, was I indeed even now being held as his hostage? I knew the answer to none of these things; and not a glimmer could I gain from "Mad-boy" McCammond, whom I taxed all day with my questions and whose features I sought again now in search of some possible, unguarded clue.

There was nothing to be discerned. He sat, a little ruffled maybe through a surfeit of food and wine, but still erect, rather formal and unlike the "Mad-boy" I had known of old, keeping an obvious tight rein on his state of sobriety. He was uniformed in undress order of light field grey, and his tunic, with epaulets bearing the Chinese insignia of a General, had obviously been cut with precision. On his breast hung three medals; the first two were rewards for service with the Marshal; the third he had gained in some minor British operation during the early 'twenties, not long after he had been gazetted from Sandhurst; and it was strange indeed to see the Military Cross worn in the wake of such odd companions. Two other things I noticed about the young Irishman that evening: he wore a revolver at the ready in its holster and his eyes seemed but seldom to stray from the Marshal.

There was little to note about "Danny" before he slumped into a heap on the floor and was left there to the utter unconcern of the others. He had been in the air all day, no doubt after a long night occupied in making up for lost time among the brighter haunts of Shanghai. I put him down as being a typical young American of the dare-devil type to whom life, in its probable brevity, existed as a prolonged escapade. He could hardly have been more than twenty-four and the only embellishments his tunic bore were miniature wings and evidence that he held the rank of full Colonel.

Then there was Major-General Huang who was the Warlord's Chief of Staff. Ralph Huang was a product of Harrow and "The Shop" and in every way a delightful fellow with the unusual faculty of combining the best qualities of both the East and West. There could be no question concerning his genuine respect for the Marshal, indeed it was impossible to be other than aware that he worshipped his War-lord even more deeply than did "Mad-boy". The difference probably amounted to no more than the fact that the Irishman did at times have occasional thoughts for himself.

The party was completed by Dr. Chen, a somewhat sinister man who wore wide horn-rimmed glasses and a long black gown. He was the Marshal's "Minister for Civil affairs" and had just returned to the *Yamen* that day, having completed an extended tour, lasting through several months, during which he had visited every town and district within the wide territories where the War-lord's rule held sway. Dr. Chen became more and more expansive as the night wore on; and, in the end, his timely return to the *Yamen* developed a significance which, for me, was deep in the extreme, since it provided an answer to one

at least among my questions. It was Dr. Chen's proud boast
that the success of his recent mission lay in the fact that he had
brought sufficient pressure to bear upon a vast and widely-
scattered populace to extract from them, *in advance,* their taxes
falling due over the next ten years. He was no more specific
than to state that the necessity for such ruthless action lay in the
interests of provincial developments which would ultimately
benefit the people themselves.

So much did Dr. Chen say to me: to the thousands whose
"benefit" would amount to no more than immediate starva-
tion, I had a notion that he had not said "developments" but
"roads".

"I must turn to the highways," the Marshal had said, "to
deaden the attention of my troops to the rebellious elements":
I understood *now* what he meant. "Roads" was a Face-saving
figure of speech, no more than a means to an end. The over-
taxed peasant must perish, I thought; but I doubted, as he died
slowly and in desperate want, he would suffer the less
by knowing that his life was token for the loyalty of a
soldier.

The orgy of eating had terminated with the traditional bowls
of rice and tea; but while the Marshal remained on the crest of
his form, in a mood of ever-increasing benevolence, no question
arose of forsaking the table. The War-lord, who periodically
wiped his glowing face with a steaming towel had consumed,
without the aid of the others, a full flagon of native liquor, and
was now surveying, with relish, a second, which he insisted
upon opening himself by the simple expedient of breaking its
neck on the back of my chair. He offered me a share in this;
but knowing the immediate effect that such a travesty of

brandy would impose upon an already discomfited stomach I craved, most courteously, to be excused: the Marshal, despite his earlier designs so obviously aimed at seeing me "spliced", seemed now less inclined to insist. Ralph Huang was aware of the reason, which he whispered in a neutral tongue: "*c'est la dernière bouteille dans la cave*".

"Marshal Meng," I presently began, with a view to some expression of thanks to a lavish host; but he raised his disengaged hand in objection.

"I would like it," he said, "if you address me more familiarly by the honourable name which was given to him who was once the Marshal Meng of England."

During this stage of the proceedings the War-lord, not a little surprisingly, was suffering from hiccoughs which were unleashed at intervals upon his audience with a deafening lack of restraint.

"Of England?" I repeated in a bewildered voice.

"*Ker-cher-na*," he announced whilst in the throes of an internal upheaval which expelled itself like a clap of thunder re-echoing back from the rafters.

"Mad-boy" took the opportunity of mouthing across at me "Kitchener—he's after asking you to be calling him 'Herbert';" at which astonishing prompt I have no doubt my already bemused expression would become the look of a lunatic. But, if indeed it was the Marshal's wish, then . . .

"Look here, Herbert . . ." I began, accidentally slipping back into English: but that was as far as I got before stranger events began really to happen in earnest.

The door opened and an officer of the *Yamen* Guard approached the Marshal. "It is an hour before dawn," he announced. "Your Excellency wished to speak with the rebels before they bow to the sword."

In a moment the War-lord was steady and his clear voice penetrated the stillness of the room.

"Bring them before me now."

As the officer went about his bidding there was a stifled gasp followed by the scamper of feet and, though my eyes were held to the Marshal, I was aware that the girls had hurriedly left through the servants' door. Then I heard the nervous tones of Dr. Chen excusing himself on some hastily-framed pretext and I knew that he must be lily-livered too. So only the three of us, Ralph Huang, "Mad-boy" and I, remained seated by the Marshal as the main door opened again to admit, with their guards, six men whose heads were shortly due to be severed.

They were a strangely assorted lot; one was outstanding in his physical bearing and fearless expression and in particular contrast to another—who looked no more than a boy of fifteen —upon whom terror had taken a merciless grip; the remaining four were nondescript rabble. All were stripped to the waist, their wrists manacled and each had been branded on the chest with the indelible legend of "Traitor". They knelt in line and bowed their heads before the Marshal. Meng Li Fu then rose, poised in perfect dignity, bowed in turn to them and bade the guards unshackle the men and then withdraw. Presently, in slow steady tones of quiet authority, he addressed himself to the condemned.

"I know each of you," he began, "by name and to be emissaries from the armies of others who would barter for the loyalty of my troops. I know also," he went on, "from whence you each have come and to where I shall shortly return your

187

severed heads, whilst your bodies remain rotting above the soil.
I offer you no quarter, for your kidney is such as calls for none:
but as an honourable soldier I will grant to your elected spokesman the usual courtesy which is the last privilege of speaking at
will from the heart. Please stand to your feet."

The Marshal then seated himself and the branded men all
rose with the exception of the whimpering boy who remained
kneeling and pleading most pitifully for mercy.

"High *Tuchan*—I am no rebel, no traitor. Justice," he cried,
"has forsaken me. Oh my Lord I have served none but you . . .
none—never . . ." then he broke down so completely in a
torrent of sobbing that I was moved, irresistibly, to the point
of intervention.

"Your Excellency," I said rising, "this is none of my affair;
but permit me to suggest that the boy seems over-young to
have part in such troubles as these."

It had to come out; though I, whose business it should have
been to remain silent, nervously watched the Marshal's face
with a sense of grave misgiving. His features, mask-like and
immovable, cast a contemptuous glance at the squirming youth:
then, to my intense surprise, he gently commanded the boy to
rise, to be silent and to stand apart from the others.

"My honoured guest, the Englishman," he added, "presumes
to say you are innocent. For his sake, therefore, I will spare you
the headman's sword." He turned to face the others. "I now
await the words that would spring from the spokesman's
heart."

The words then came from the one of broad stature and
fearless expression.

"High *Tuchan*," he began with a gracious bow, "first I

speak, not as a common soldier under arms to the Lord of the Elegant Sword; but as a Captain in the Nanking company of Guards whose allegiance is to the Marshal Chiang. And, since you have extended to me the last liberty of speaking from the heart, I would say, High *Tuchan*, that I am an actor of equal talent with you."

In the unbearable silence which followed this opening, I was conscious that "Mad-boy's" hand moved instinctively towards his holster.

"You said just now," continued the Captain, "that you pose as an honourable soldier. You are an able and fearless one—yes; but I say that he who one days wears the insignia which proclaims him a Marshal of China; and on the next is to be seen in the guise of some mute, mild mercenary, so as to spy upon his restless and unpaid men, can never, at least in the code of the Central Armies, be considered a soldier of honour."

Again I was aware of "Mad-boy" shifting his feet as his hand took a grip on the butt of his revolver.

The spokesman now concluded: "I will use my last words in the expression of thanks for the patient ear so graciously afforded me. In return for this, I will extend to you the gift of some knowledge that may be of service in your private affairs. Among your *Yamen* Guard and in all the Garrisons which house so many who may shortly desert your arms, it is everywhere known that the mute Lao Er has the same brave eyes as the Marshal Meng Li Fu."

He bowed elegantly and was silent.

Then, with a wealth of deliberation and in all his assembled dignity, the Marshal rose and, with a gesture of courtesy, began his answer to this outspoken address:

"Captain Yang—for I have indeed been aware as to your identity—you are the fearless son of a proud father whom I once knew to be the Provincial Governor of Northern Hupeh. I can never be as proud as he, for in the matter of a son I am so much the far less fortunate. It is for this reason that I have never betrayed the fact that mine be the mute and sickly half-wit whom I have none the less dearly loved and kept for ever, close at hand. I pray that you may forbear to taunt an ageing man who speaks thus humbly in his hour of desperate grief: that you will not torture me the more by an insistence that I now should send for my son to prove that my words are true. You see . . ." and it was as if the Marshal's eyes, now brimful with unchecked tears, reached out towards the stars, "you see, poor creature though he may have been, my son was abundantly dear to me —and he died this afternoon. That is all there is to be said."

Even the men whom he had condemned were moved beyond further words by the Marshal's genuine expressions of grief. His was the curtain; he had seen to it that his must be the last lines spoken in this strange, unaccountable drama. And presently, as though it were to clear the stage and change the set, the guards returned, and led the six men out to meet—all but one—their ignominious end.

The Marshal wiped his face; then seizing the flagon of brandy, he raised its jagged neck to his lips and, throwing back his head, drained its contents in a single audible gulp.

"Your son . . ." I began presently, since I was curious to know how a man so remarkable might respond. "Through what means did he die?"

The Marshal turned himself fully towards me and soon his

whole countenance was beaming in obvious delight at my question.

"He died," he replied, "on the Highway."

Then his whole frame shook in a paroxysm of hiccoughs and uncontrolled mirth.

Eventually he rose and for a moment his stance was unsteady. "Come," he said, "it is dawn with over-much death in the air; and an Actor, like a Marshal, tends to grow weary."

We all automatically rose and moved from the table, while the War-lord, with his hand on my sleeve, went on, "I must thank you for honouring me with your distinguished company and, indeed, I am sorry that it will not now be necessary for your visit to be further prolonged. The American Colonel—if you wish it—will fly you back to your Treaty port to-morrow or . . ." he paused and looked about him. "General Huang— where *is* the American Colonel ? "

Ralph Huang could hardly suppress a smile as he nodded at the Marshal's feet where lay the recumbent figure of "Danny" in an attitude of deep and drunken slumber.

"*Ai Ya!*" exclaimed the War-lord, fearful lest at an earlier hour he had unaccountably slaughtered his pilot. Hurriedly and as though to make certain, he unsheathed his sword and drove its tip fully an inch into the fleshier part of the American's buttock.

Danny came-to with a yell, which gave complete satisfaction to the Marshal who merely nodded, put up his sword and made for the door.

Ralph Huang and "Mad-boy" stood strictly to attention and bowed but perceptibly as the War-lord, with stately carriage and grave dignity, moved out between them. So he passed from view through the door and out of my immediate, since emptier, life.

But fortunate indeed are such as I, whose walls of memory are richly adorned by the colours and contrasts of so many a Chinese canvas: and most remarkable among them all in vivid reflection is the portrait of a War-lord with an inscrutable look upon a strangely elegant face.

.   .   .   .   .   .

XIII

RETURN TO EDEN

IN the spring of 1945 I spent a week-end at that famous rendezvous of North-country anglers—the Mitre Hotel at Wichell—overlooking the wide expanse of sloping woods below Harby Castle which reach down to the grey-clear and effortlessly-moving waters of the river Eden. Here is a paradise for those who would cast a fly towards the ripple of a rising salmon: but I had been drawn more urgently by the coercing call of nostalgia back to a boyhood haunt. While new missiles of annihilation fell haphazardly about London, I sought brief sanctuary in rural beauty by the loveliest stretch of woods and water which, in many years of roaming about the world, I yet found unsurpassed.

New folk had come to the village and it seemed that my old friends were gone: what I had known as an inn was a flourishing State-managed hotel, its erstwhile stables converted into a garage: a half-hourly 'bus service brought its week-end litter to the glades: and I was a stranger after the passing of well-nigh four decades. But there was the rough green with its ancient commemorative cross and about it the picturesque diversity of dwellings had, for the most part, changed no more than in their tenantry: the Norman tower, successor of centuries ago to an earlier Saxon edifice, still rose above the ivied church—sole testimony in a decaying age to a steadfast and changeless Faith:

and, older than history, as yet unhewn, were the deep, lush woods below, that flanked on either side the soft, rippling curves of the river. To all these I was no stranger: no more than a man may be to his mother or indeed, ever, to the sights and sounds and the early springtide of his first environment. Basking in the gentle glow of this reflection and in the noon stillness of an April Sunday, I strolled past "The Old House", and leisurely along by the village green, knowing that my footsteps would lead me down the steep slope, past the lych-gate by the church and inevitably on to the waters of the Eden.

Then I paused awhile as my thoughts were distracted by what was at first the trickle, then the small stream, of villagers and visitors who came towards me, homeward-bound from Sunday morning service. Some passed by in motor-cars, to whom I paid no heed: they would be domiciled further afield. It was a local face I sought; one, or perhaps more, that might not, in nearly two-score years, have mellowed beyond recognition. But all were unknown to me, as indeed, obviously I was to them.

Then, at the end of the procession walked two young men together, both of whom looked to be under twenty, and who, although they did not present what I was looking for, could not but demand my undivided attention for a variety of reasons. They were both magnificently built, which counteracted any impression of their height—which I judged to be about six and a half feet—making them appear excessively tall. They each bore the same clean, clear-cut, rather sensitive features which were so alike as to deny any doubts as to their relationship. But in the matter of their dress they presented not only a strange contrast to this rural setting, but were, I suppose, an exact and indeed somewhat unconventional antithesis to one another. One wore, as it were a tight glove, his superbly-tailored khaki service jacket with its highly-polished buttons arranged in clusters of three; his shoes and belt had the sheen of rich mahogany, whilst nigh touching the bridge of his nose was the gilt-edged peak of his blue hat with its large silver badge and its band of "dice-board": a single star on each shoulder proclaimed him to be an ensign in the Scots Guards. The other, who walked with his counter-part, bore himself with a no less unaffected swagger, and, with no "flat-a-back" about the angle of his cap, lent becoming credit to the "square-rig" and "bell-bottomed" trousers of the lower deck. I stood there, lost to all else, fascinated by their appearance and by the spectacle in a Cumberland village of an officer in the Brigade marching along with a matelot who could hardly have been other than his identical twin.

As they approached me, absorbed by each other in gay conversation, I was overwhelmed by a curious desire to know who they might be, and how, and when, they had come to live here—if indeed they did—and a number of other things about them as well, including the quite inconsequent consideration as to whether they had ever thought of changing uniforms and confounding their friends.

"Excuse me butting in," I started rather limply, looking up under the "cheese-cutter" that towered over me as they passed by; "but at one time I had quite a few friends in your regiment; I was wondering if you knew . . ."

His keen young eye regarded me critically as he, and his carbon-copy in bell-bottoms halted abruptly in their tracks:

but when I mentioned the name his face lit up and he said immediately. "Oh yes, sir. Colonel John"—his glance swivelled round to the solitary star on his shoulder—"frightfully senior of course," he added with a smile; and I was struck afresh by the way that junior officers in the Brigade invariably refer to their seniors by their Christian names until the latter become Colonels or Generals, when the familiarity is retained but with the additional prefix of rank.

"And have you come across . . ." I mentioned the name of a boy whose father I had first met when he was an attaché in Peking.

"David!" he exclaimed jubilantly. "But he's my greatest friend; always has been—that is, discounting this hairy matelot here. David was at school, then at Caterham and Pirbright with me; we passed out together at Mons—he got the belt: we've been up at Hawick but are going overseas on Tuesday. But I was forgetting; I knew David first as an infant in China."

"In China!" I exclaimed. It instantly struck me that this terrific specimen of young guards officer seemed somehow even more remote from any association with China than he did with this quiet corner of Cumberland. But I realised by his afterthought that we could no doubt discover a host more among mutual acquaintances.

"That's intensely interesting to me," I added, and suggested that the two of them should come back to "The Mitre" with me and have a drink. It was the sailor who demurred, explaining that they were both on short embarkation leave and their grandparents, with whom they were staying, would be expecting them.

"But, sir," he added, "if you would care to come in—the house is just here—I know they both would be delighted. Why not stay to lunch?"

I was struck now not only by their appearance but by their charming manners; and perhaps rather too eagerly accepted. The young soldier said, "Excellent show—come on," and we moved off, I walking between them and feeling that my five feet eleven and a half had shrunk to a mere four foot nothing.

"I'm Nigel," said the same voice, emanating from somewhere considerably above the thin patch on my crown; "and the Senior Service on your left is rightly represented by my one-day-older brother who is Anthony. Here is the gate: forgive us if we do a lightning change; we only parade like this for Church—you know, sir—the old people rather expect it. Choose the dry sherry, it's better than the medium . . ."

" 'The Old House'," I observed, trying to conceal my excitement. "How long have your grandparents lived here?"

"Oh—about ten years, I suppose," came the reply as we walked up the gravel drive to the front door. "They moved here from the South just after we came home to School."

I realised that as they had come from another district I would not have known them in my time which was fully confirmed by my first eager glance at the charming and very handsome elderly couple who greeted us at the door. Here I was left to introduce myself, since the moment the boys reached the hall they did no more than mutter something quite inaudible in polite reference to me before their caps were thrown on to a camphor chest and they bounded upstairs after one another, shouting "Off with the Motley!" and undoing buttons and straps as they went.

"Steady, there!" implored their Grandfather after them. "You'll have the house down on top of us."

"What wonderful chaps they are," I remarked. "By the way, they were kind enough to ask me in. I hope you don't mind. I'm afraid none of us know each other's names. Mine is . . ."

My attempt to give expression to the formalities was immediately swept aside with a laugh and an unmistakable welcome towards a cheerful log fire and two decanters of sherry.

"They're quite hopeless," remarked their Grandmother, with an amused yet quite obvious expression of deep affection on her face. "We are delighted you should come." And I sensed that, while the boys were staying here, nothing else very much mattered.

"Are they here often?" I enquired.

"Oh, yes," she replied. "We've more or less brought them up since they were eight. You see—their parents, my son and his wife, are abroad . . ."

"Dry or medium?" interposed their Grandfather, fingering a decanter and wincing only slightly as what sounded like a heavy boot being flung from a height on the floor above rattled the chandelier under which he was standing.

"Dry if I may, please. Odd," I went on, "that twins should choose different services."

Their Grandfather was in the midst of explaining that they were different in many ways when he was interrupted by a series of violent leaps on the floor above which instinctively caused him to screw up his features and draw his chair slightly further out of range from the centre of the ceiling.

"For instance," his wife explained for my benefit, "Anthony sits on his bed and draws his trousers on delicately. Nigel invariably jumps into his! It's always been the same. Won't you stay for luncheon?"

I must have appeared excessively rude by not immediately acknowledging her kindness, but something had suddenly flashed back to me and my mind was concentrating on events which had happened nineteen years earlier as my attention was focused on a photograph that stood in a silver frame above the writing desk. I was not aware that my hostess's eyes must have followed mine until she remarked quietly.

"She's very lovely—don't you think? That was taken many years ago: but only the last three may have changed her, though we hope . . ." She cleared her throat. "She is the twins' Mother of course. Our son and she were on their way home from China at the beginning of 1942 and were caught in Manila after Pearl Harbour: They are in Santa Lucia internment camp —that's all we know: not very healthy we hear; the Japanese can be a bit brutal . . .

"I'm terribly sorry," I said, hurriedly. "I . . ."

"But we must forget it," she went on, "especially when the boys are home and both of them just going overseas." She turned to me and smiled a little wearily. "We try not to think about that either: everyone's got their little troubles and after all we escape quite a lot up here. I only mentioned it because you were looking at that photograph and she—poor girl—has had more than her share: it started when the twins were born . . ."

There was a crash in the hall outside, immediately followed by another, and as their Grandfather turned up the lapels of his coat and drew his head downwards, I knew that the boys had each cleared the last flight of stairs, from a standing jump. They were with us now, quite indistinguishable to me, towering like a couple of giants above the lintel of the door, clad in the most disreputable country clothes, and almost bursting, it seemed, with the rich glow of fitness and health.

"Grannie—are the big eats laid on—we're starving," said one.

"But *famished*," echoed the other.

"Yes; tell Bessie," came the soft rejoinder. "Listen: tell Bessie to lay an extra place and then we're ready."

As they scrambled towards the back premises I made mild protest only to be met with the whispered reassurance, "It's all right: I've been hoarding a ham, but they don't know yet: you see it's the last day they'll . . ."

I am afraid that the rest of her sentence was lost, for as the war-cries echoed along the passage I was no longer able to contain myself.

"You were saying when the twins were born," I reminded her, vainly endeavouring to control my excitement. "It is almost inconceivable how these coincidences occur, but the mention of China, of the names Anthony and Nigel, the day's difference in their ages and finally the photograph of their Mother which ties it all together have convinced me of something. Just," I concluded, "to be finally certain—I apologise for not catching it—but surely your name must be Forsythe."

"Of course it's Forsythe," broke in the old man, emerging from his coat collar and regarding me closely. "Have you some news . . ."

"My news," I replied, "is no more than ancient history, but it has a bearing on the present. First, sir, I must ask if you have ever heard the tale of adventures that attended, then followed, the arrival into this world of those two giants, Anthony and Nigel, neither of whom weighed as much as four pounds at birth, and how fortunate they are to be alive and how almost incredible it seems that they have grown to such dimensions. Have you heard?"

The old man sat a little more upright in his chair and his wife leaned a little nearer towards me.

"Only," he countered, "that they were born long before they were expected, in a hill station, or on a train or something, and there was trouble of a sort—one of these Chinese rebellions, if I remember. The boy was away exploring in the wilds at the time, not expecting anything to happen for a coupla' months: and the girl—well she's never said very much . . ."

"She wouldn't," I observed. Then rising, I picked up the photograph in the silver frame and turned to the two of them who were now regarding me with an air of interest and expectancy.

"Sir, and with your permission, Mrs. Forsythe," I said, "you should *all* know the story, for I feel convinced that if I relate it, none of you will worry overmuch, or any more, about the twins' Mother in Santa Lucia camp. This girl, though her looks belie it, is not only the toughest, but quite the bravest woman I know. My part in that drama was infinitesimal compared to hers. I merely ran ten miles over the hills to find a doctor—and again two days later to find a padre to christen those two frail bundles of practically nothing, before they had to run the gauntlet of opposing armies. To me it was no more than a dramatic adventure and always a race against time—but for her—forgive me—but Good God! this girl could go through hell without turning a hair and come out of it quite unscathed. None of you need worry on her behalf—not for a moment— ever . . ."

The gong echoed through the old house and there was laughter and scurrying footsteps in the hall. Mrs. Forsythe rose and put her hand on mine. "Tell all of us," she said softly, "it'll be most interesting: but shall we tackle 'the big eats' first?"

Then she led the way into the dining room.

.   .   .   .

During the mid-summer of 1926 whilst I was stationed in the humid climate of the Yangtze valley, I succumbed to a bout of malaria and was subsequently ordered away from Hankow to recuperate for a full week at Mei-shan, a small resort situated in the hills of South Honan, some sixty miles distant. The idea would hardly have appealed to me at the best of times, for the place consisted of no more than a few widely-scattered bungalows and a guest house, which served as a cooler retreat for British and American wives, with their children, whose menfolk were wont to join them only at week-ends. At this time, in particular, the idea appealed to me still less, for things were afoot which would seem to demand the presence at their posts of all responsible Britons.

The three cities of the Central Yangste, known collectively as Wu-han, were under immediate threat of capture by the advancing Red armies led by a then-unknown young soldier called Chiang Kai-shek, who was later destined to spend over twenty years fighting against them. Among the slogans employed by this conquering force, which was sweeping up from the South, were "Down with Imperialism"; "Abolish the unequal Treaties" and even extended to exhortations in mob harangue to force out the foreigner and seize his property. It seemed no time to be leaving Hankow, principal of the Wuhan cities and a Treaty port with a large and prosperous British Concession protected by no more than a cruiser and a gun-boat anchored off the Bund, two platoons of Royal Marines and the local volunteers recruited from foreign business representatives such as myself.

The fact that the British territory was subsequently overrun, the Marines withdrawn, the Volunteers disbanded and the Union Jack openly insulted, while the Concession was meekly handed over at the behest of an apathetic Whitehall, is no more than a now-forgotten page of history concerned with the decline of British prestige abroad during the past twenty-five years. But it serves here only to illustrate an atmosphere in which the lives and property of English men and women were of little account to the crude warring factions involved on the spot, and apparently of no great concern to those who sat in comfortable officialdom at home.

Had I known that events were to follow with such unexpected suddenness I would have disobeyed orders and stayed in Hankow: but, as it was, I travelled the sixty miles North to Sin-Tien station on the Peking-Hankow railway from where I was borne in a wicker chair up the steep three-mile track that led to Mei-shan. There, remote from communication with the outside world, I was prepared to stay no more than a week, somewhat self-consciously a lone able-bodied male amongst a host of women and children in a rather ramshackle and over-crowded guest-house.

On the second night of my visit the most violent thunder-storm broke over the wide range of hills surrounding us, the fury of which became the more eerie through the frightened screams of children within the house and the baying of the pariah dogs who sought shelter without. At the height of the storm, and as the rain streamed down in torrents outside my room I thought I heard a woman's voice calling in urgent tones below my window and endeavouring to be heard above the tumult. I threw up the sash and as I did so an almost blinding flash of lightning revealed the bedraggled and drenched figure of a young American wife I knew, clutching a hurricane lamp and appealing to me to come quickly. I threw on a few clothes and an old trench-coat, and within a few seconds I had let her into the hall.

"Stella—what on earth . . ." I began.

"There's no time to waste," she said urgently; "it's a doctor and a nurse quickly: I'm sharing a bungalow with Kitty Forsythe and she's starting to have a baby . . ."

"Good God!" I exclaimed. "There's no-one in this place." I thought frantically, "but wait a minute, there's Mrs. James who runs this joint. I think she *was* a nurse . . ."

"Well, for heaven's sake get her quickly."

I ran along and hammered on Sophie James's door, hoping to make myself heard above the unceasing clamour of the storm. Presently I had informed her what was happening in the nearest bungalow. She was a brick, that woman, if ever there was one: said she'd never been present at any birth except her own, and that all her nursing had been done in Army wards during the war; but she'd pack some things and go along right away, and in the meantime Stella must remove those soaking clothes and have her bed.

"I know everyone who's in Mei-shan at the moment," she went on, "and there's no one else—certainly no midwife—so it looks as if you and I will have to tackle this job between us."

"Me!" I said, trying to conceal my horror.

"Oh, your part's easy," she assured me. "You have only to find your way to the Inland Mission hostel and bring back a doctor as fast as your legs will carry you. If only there were telephones; but if you keep to the right track it can't be more than ten miles . . . Here, take this hurricane lamp; and Stella, you come along to my room."

I had discarded my sopping trench-coat and hidden it with the lamp under a bush (which I never succeeded in rediscovering) when the storm passed and dawn broke suddenly. I cursed my lack of training and recent bout of sickness as I cantered the last two miles of my journey in an open shirt and shorts and a pair of canvas shoes which continually seemed to be taking in fresh supplies of sand and gravel. I was grateful for my good fortune in finding the way, and even more so for the manner of my reception at the Inland Mission Summer Hostel, where, though it was before six in the morning, all appeared to be up and about. They insisted I must eat and rest; and indeed, to my impatience, seemed more concerned about me than the urgent object of my journey

"Babies," one of them said, "are born in China, prematurely and otherwise, at the rate of well over a thousand an hour without much fuss or preparation. It is a natural function . . ."

"Yes, but . . ."

"You look as if you'd got a touch of malaria . . ."

It was no use protesting; I had to suffer being given some dope which certainly refreshed me: but I felt that precious minutes were slipping by and was not happy until I was shortly urging on the sluggish ass that had been rounded up, with another of its kind, to convey the doctor and me back to Mei-shan.

"Damn!" unexpectedly exclaimed my companion, in somewhat unmissionary parlance nearly two hours later as we trotted along within half a mile of the bungalow. "I've forgotten the blasted anaesthetic."

Sophie James met us at the door.

"How is she?" I began.

"Wonderful! Truly marvellous," was the reply. "Doctor, would you like to come along?"

Within five minutes he rejoined me on the mound of rough scrub across the pathway.

"In oodles of time," he remarked. "By the way, d'you know her?"

I shook my head. "Think I met her husband once; he goes off into the Gobi looking for eggs, or something." Then we smoked and sat in silence for a time.

"Funny thing," he observed presently. "I did my stuff at 'Bart's' years ago, of course—but I've never attended an English woman before—not for this sort of thing, I mean."

I was almost asleep when I suddenly remembered something and sat up.

"What about that anaesthetic?" I asked. "Shall I go back?"

"On no, that's all right," he replied. "Mrs. What's-her-name, the nurse woman, has sent her Chinese cook over on one of the donkeys."

"Then it's all right if I go and get some shut-eye?"

"You'd better," he advised, "and I'll see about somebody pumping up a drop of water—ought to get it on the boil . . ."

.   .   .   .   .   .

It was after seven in the evening when I awoke and the news was already abroad that less than an hour earlier Mrs. Forsythe had given birth to a boy. The event was really no immediate concern of mine, but I found it impossible to escape some feeling of apprehension when I walked out in the cool evening air and observed Mrs. James's cook astride the animal which had earlier borne me in the same direction, leisurely ambling towards the bungalow with a package in train. That girl must have had a hell of a time, I thought.

I realised the next morning that my sentiment was fully justified: another boy had been born half an hour after midnight.

There was nothing suitably available with which to put it to the test, but the doctor calculated that the infants would probably not weigh as much as seven and a half pounds between them. Neither he, nor the ex-army nurse, were in any way fully qualified or up-to-date in the science of the miracle which they had performed, but they had managed to bring it off, so far successfully, with hardly the aid of a single amenity which would normally be available in the meanest English household.

I glanced at the little man whose sparse frame was drooping through anxiety and fatigue. Then spontaneously, and for no reason other than that I had suddenly developed a profound admiration for him, I wrung his hand and said, "You ought to be proud . . ."

"Oh—I'm getting quite good at it now," was all that medical missionary would say in acknowledgement; "but," he added, "it's that young Mother who deserves all the praise: I'll wager that no mere man could ever have lived out the time she's been through; and yet she's lying in there now, as happy as Larry, and just as proud of those boys as though they were a couple of giants."

"I hope they will be, someday," I said; then added rather tentatively, "are they all right?"

"About a fifty-fifty chance," he replied. "I've sent word back to the Hostel asking them to arrange for a fully-qualified nurse and some equipment to be sent up from the Mission Hospital in Hankow. In the meantime I'll stand by here and Mrs. James and I'll do all that's possible. The mother's sheer strength of will should see her through all right and the boys stand a fair chance—provided, of course," he concluded, "nothing unforeseen happens."

. . . .

The unforeseen did happen at five o'clock two mornings later.

I was rudely awakened on this occasion by one of the junior British Consulate staff from Hankow.

"We've got to get moving right away," he urged.

"Who—where?" I asked, sitting up.

"Everyone—all these women and children here—the missionaries too, wherever they are. It's got to be done right away otherwise anything may happen and the 'C.G.' cannot accept responsibility. Look here," he went on rather breathlessly, "while you're pulling on some clothes I'll tell you the position. Briefly it's like this: Chiang Kai-shek's troops are in Hanyang and literally at the gates of Hankow and demonstrations are already taking place at the boundaries of the Concession. Marshal Wu Pei Fu told the 'C.G.' last night that he can hold on to the city no longer than a further forty-eight hours, if that. It's all the time we've got to get the women and children out of here, down to Hankow and aboard the ships."

I was feverishly drawing on a pair of shorts, still slightly bewildered.

"Aren't they safer *here* than in Hankow?" I ventured.

"Safer! Listen: Marshal Wu has sent a special train to Sin-Tien; I came up in it: it's waiting down there now. He's done it at the instigation of the 'C.G.' to give these people a chance. You see, when the Marshal gives up Hankow he has elected to withdraw his army here—*here* to Mei-shan, and stem the Red's advance towards Peking. Don't you understand—this is the day-after-tomorrow's battlefield . . ."

"Wait a minute," I said. "Oughtn't we to take them North?"

"My instructions are quite clear," he replied. "Besides the Yellow river bridge . . ."

I was half way into a light pull-over when I suddenly remembered.

"Good God!" I exclaimed, and sat down on my bed.

"For heaven's sake get a move on," said the other. "We've no time . . ."

"When has the train got to leave?" I asked.

"No later than five this evening—that's twelve hours from now. The evacuation ship is sailing at midnight."

"All right," I said. "The house-boy will wake everybody here and tell them to get ready. You must explain things—tactfully, of course, if the kids are about—and then get somebody to take you round all the bungalows—all of them where there are foreigners staying—except the nearest one and I'll deal with that myself, right away."

Then I went over and stirred the little missionary doctor, who was sleeping fully clothed on the open verandah of Mrs. Forsythe's bungalow, and told him the news. When he grasped the full significance of it, a cloud came over his normally unruffled countenance and he disappeared inside the door to confer with Sophie James.

After about five minutes they both emerged and indicated that Mrs. Forsythe would like to see me.

I found her, propped up on pillows, and if her face betrayed any manifestation of physical strain this was entirely outlawed by an unutterably lovely radiance that absorbed every feature. Within her reach were the two halves of a wicker hamper, each of which housed in snug repose quite the tiniest people I had ever seen.

"Aren't they darlings," she remarked, then turning to me, "I've never met you," she said, "I only know you've been terribly kind and that's all the more reason why I wanted to thank you for what you did. It was grand of you."

I murmured something before she went on.

"So now we've got to strike camp?"

"Can it be done?" I asked. "Otherwise I'm quite ready to . . ."

"There would seem no option," she replied.

A frail, rather delicate, hand emerged from the bedclothes and was laid on mine.

"We'll have to try," she continued, "but I'm afraid we must rely on you again: I wonder—can I ask you? You see—I don't worry about myself: but my sons—they're such tiny little chaps—I would like somebody to christen them first—you know—just in case . . ."

I had to swallow hard before I could re-assure her that somehow it would be arranged: and then I left hurriedly, biting back a weak tendency to emotion and a thousand curses upon the wretched consequences of man's barbarity. With no great sense of chivalry or heroics I just knew that there was the one woman I'd cheerfully die for.

It was nearly mid-day before I returned, pretty well all in, from the far-away Mission Hostel, accompanied by a stalwart in light clerical garb who had won the half-mile for Cambridge in 1909. Mei-shan was deserted, save for the small party gathered at the bungalow, which included the Doctor, Sophie James and Stella, who with me stood sponsor at the little ceremony devoted to Anthony and Nigel.

But there were the chair-coolies waiting by the mound opposite, and it was close on five o'clock by the time, after innumerable halts for necessary respite, we completed the hazardous journey down to Sin-Tien station. There, the doctor and the padre insisted on accompanying me on to the train with every intention of returning to their Mission only when the personal crisis was over and the party free from danger. They, like Kitty Forsythe, who, with her sons and Mrs. James, were in possession of the next compartment; had nothing but the most ultimate thoughts for their own security.

About an hour later the train slowly pulled out South, along the single track towards Hankow.

It must have been nearly nine in the evening before our slow journey terminated in an abrupt halt and it was growing dark when the consular representative and I walked along the line to discover that the locomotive which had been drawing the train now steadfastly refused to budge an inch further. We were still twenty miles away from our destination and if we were delayed much longer I had a fear that some of our passengers might develop a tendency to become panic-stricken. Then a series of things happened which I must confess brought more than a momentary panic to me.

A lever-driven trolley came round a bend in the line towards us with four pairs of Chinese hands propelling it at top speed. An English official of the railway who was accompanying it, had the presence of mind to leap off the vehicle in time and it was fortunate for them that the others did the same, before it hit the bumpers of our engine with terrific impact. But the Englishman lost no time in picking himself up: he was obviously a man with not a moment to lose.

"*Wei-tzo! Wei-tzo! Kwei-kwei wei-tzo!*" he urged the driver of our train. "Get back! Get back! Quickly!" he repeated in English.

Spontaneously the alarmed Chinese in the cab swung the lever over to reverse and with a wheeze, accompanied by a great outpouring of steam, the train which had refused to proceed forward—through some miracle—moved back. We reached a siding and the points were switched over again with no more than moments to spare.

We could hear their approach for miles in the still gathering dusk and we stood on the embankment waiting with feelings of awe and apprehension in the knowledge (which we silently prayed our restless passengers might not share) that Hankow had fallen and that a defeated army was being swiftly born towards us in a wild stampede to the North.

I shall not easily forget the macabre sight of those monster trains urging past us in the half light. No less than a hundred and eighty open waggons, half of them set with bell tents, the rest loaded with guns and equipment, were drawn in one unit by four powerful locomotives which belched forth furnace-lit clouds of grey smoke and sparks which flew high into the dusk, while on the couplings of the foremost hung the splintered wreckage of the lever-driven trolley. Less than a mile behind came another of similar dimensions, then another, followed by yet one more seemingly even of greater magnitude and thundering past at higher speed than its forerunners. Then from away up the line to the North there came back to us a vivid flash, followed by a noise which there could be no mistaking. It was the simultaneous impact of a hundred metal buffers: and we knew that calamity was not far distant and the chance of our party ever reaching sanctuary or of the continued existence of Anthony and Nigel had become swiftly charged with fresh doubts and any means of escape from our predicament seemed hopelessly remote.

On hearing the crash, the railway official was the first to leap into action and, with a quickness apparent in both mind and

213

body, he seized a red lamp from the guard and tore off down the track. He had the brave and unhesitating intention of waving to a stop any further mass units that might be following up. In retrospect the grimness of the situation assumes a lighter aspect at the thought of a lone Englishman flagging to a halt a train-borne Chinese Army in retreat. But nevertheless that is what he succeeded in doing and within an hour he was back, begrimed and perspiring, accompanied by two of Marshal Wu's staff officers.

They were both intellectual, if somewhat overwrought, young men, and before proceeding with the English official further along the track to take toll of the damage ahead, they advised us to evacuate the train immediately and hide somewhere in the surrounding country. Only half of Wu Pei Fu's army was to the North of us, they explained, and the remainder were about to pass us along the railway track on foot. They could not offer any guarantee for their discipline or behaviour. "Morale is pretty low among defeated troops," observed one of them, "and the Marshal will be quite unable to accept responsibility if the soldiers go through the train and take what they want. Even if they don't," he added, "now the line is blocked ahead, the Marshal may well decide to dig in here and your train will be no more than a target for both sides. It is certain," he concluded, "that, now they have taken Hankow, the Reds will come this way: if you have a hundred foreign women and children with you—then they should move away from the railway to-night, otherwise . . ."

It was just wild barren country about us, without any sign of habitation and no immediate means of obtaining either food or water which would be fit for drinking. The place was almost

unbearably humid and infested with mosquitoes. It was therefore in a decidedly unpromising atmosphere that the Consular
official, the padre and the doctor and myself held our swift
consultation. My first question concerned Kitty Forsythe.

"Not too good," was the doctor's verdict. "That journey
down the hill has used up pretty well all the strength she had."

"I see—and the twins?"

"Look here," he said, "I'm sorry I'm not very up to date as to
what might or might not be done, but you must take my
opinion for what it's worth: to shift any of them to-night would
be murder: to-morrow possibly—but not to-night."

There was silence after that for a moment as we all tried
desperately hard to think of a solution. Then it was the quiet,
authoritative tones of the padre who spoke.

"Two of us," he said, "must try and get through to Hankow
and arrange a relief party: we obviously can't follow the railroad so we must take a chance across country. I say two,
because that gives a better prospect of one getting through. The
river must be about seven or eight miles to the East of us and
there should be creeks to which a launch might be sent if we
can find one. Now I think that you"—he turned to the doctor
—"are the best man to take charge here, then you'll be close to
that young mother. I suggest you clear everyone else off the
train with all their belongings and tell them to disperse at least
a hundred yards away from the embankment and see the
mothers impress upon the kids that the slightest sound may
imperil the whole lot of them. Leave only Mrs. James on
board with Mrs. Forsythe and the twins—tell her to draw the
blinds and jam the door of the compartment. That should get
us through to-night at least. Then the remaining one amongst

the four of us must scour the countryside for food and something that's fit to drink: that is most urgent and vital, otherwise
those children will be drinking all kinds of muck. Right: now
that's all settled; which of you two are coming with me?"

"Listen," I said, "I agree, and I'm sure the rest of us do too,
with all you suggest. I think it's the only chance we've got."
The other two murmured their agreement. "*But*," I added,
"excluding the doctor who has a definite job here, the three of
us will draw lots to decide which two make for Hankow and
who goes scrounging for food."

Lots were quickly drawn and the padre and the Consular
official immediately set off and disappeared into the night
moving swiftly in a Southerly direction. I, having borrowed
all the money the others could spare, to supplement what I
already had in my possession, scrambled down the embankment to search for farms; and the doctor, who it struck me
had the toughest assignment of all, climbed back into the
train.

It was after daylight when I rejoined the party, accompanied
by two somewhat apprehensive, but richly-bribed, native boys
who had travelled miles with me, laden with chickens and eggs,
several ducks and a quantity of buffalo meat which I thought
might serve for a stew, and an assortment of vegetables. I had
also managed to acquire a few pots and pans but I had not been
very successful in the matter of precious fluids. True, I had
obtained a certain amount of milk, but that was secreted in two
bottles tied out of view round my waist and, as it subsequently
transpired, these may have played no small part in sustaining
throughout that day the lives of the twins and possibly that of
their mother as well. For water, one of my henchmen bore two

churns-full slung across his shoulder on either end of a pole; when that was finished, which I had no doubt in the heat of the day would quickly be the case, I had in mind to explore the potentialities of the engine.

I found my fellow travellers hidden from view of the railway embankment, and about half a mile away from it, scattered about the dried-up bed of a shallow creek. They were all perfectly composed and I can only relate that if any of those women knew the full portent of the imminent dangers they were facing—and the majority of them must have known it—they kept their fears to themselves and allowed no trace nor suggestion of it to extend to the children. And how those women, who normally never did a hand's turn for themselves in their own kitchens, got down to the preparation and distribution of the provisions! They organised themselves into various tasks without so much as a hint of dispute, made fires, boiled water, plucked and drew the poultry, prepared a stew pot, and, because the children outnumbered them, probably partook of but little for themselves. I left them with a profound admiration for their pluck and, hung about with the milk and delicately clutching half a dozen eggs, I made my way to the train.

An endless stream of grey-clad troops, the residue of Wu Pei Fu's army, were steadily moving North along the railway embankment and as I met the little Mission doctor I was relieved to learn that, although they had been continually passing through most of the night, they had chosen to ignore the train. It was not surprising, since it bore the appearance of being utterly deserted, as indeed it was, save for the occupants of one solitary compartment.

"Are they bearing up all right?" I asked rather anxiously.

"I'm desperately worried," he replied. "She's tried to feed them several times during the last few hours but either they won't take it, or more than likely she's got nothing to give 'em."

"I've brought some milk . . ." I began.

"You have! Good man! Where is it?"

I undid the knot under my shirt. "Here," I said, "and a few eggs."

"You're a wizard," he exclaimed with a sigh of relief.

"Good egg indeed! Now, Mrs. J. has got a spirit lamp and we'll have a boil up; then we'll give Mrs. F. breakfast and if the little brats won't eat after that, I'll serve it to 'em myself in an eye-dropper. Come on—the day may yet be saved."

As the morning wore on it became almost unbearably hot and by mid-day the atmosphere both in the train and in the unshady creek was stifling and the flies abounded in profusion. Sophie James and Stella, who took it in turns to minister to Kitty Forsythe and her sons, had stripped themselves well nigh to the last limits and were oblivious to all else save creating such comfort as they could for their charges. Only the little doctor seemed capable of remaining cool whilst fully clad even to the extent of his collar and tie and jacket. By early afternoon, when the scorching sun was at its height, the women a little distance away who struggled against mounting odds to keep the children distracted and free from a tendency to growing fears, had in the course of their exertions, long since left behind the limits of decorum demanded by a normally modest society. But I felt convinced that none would think the more of it: in heart-breaking circumstances they were behaving with a magnificent disregard for the dangers that beset them and only Kitty Forsythe deserved a little more praise than they.

I sat with her as she lay on the seat opposite, stretched across the length of the compartment and I stirred up the sparse oppressive air about her brow and face with the aid of a folded paper. Still there were little beads of perspiration about her forehead which Stella dabbed from time to time with a handkerchief soaked in Eau de Cologne. The infants in their little wicker cribs had been taken next door where Sophie James and the Doctor watched over them. The windows were open now, for the last remnants of the retreating force had passed by and there was at least respite for a while, save from the burdensome heat and the intolerable menace of the flies. Then at about five o'clock there came the rumble of big guns in the distance. Gradually they broke into their overture with growing crescendo as those from the North spoke back and some minutes later we heard the whine of the first shell.

Kitty Forsythe raised herself slightly, then sank back against the cushions which had been heavily stacked beneath her. "What a mercy it is," she breathed, "that Anthony and Nigel don't know what it's all about. Do you think . . ." she turned to me. "Do you think that the other children are all right? Oughtn't you to go and see?"

I rose and was leaving her compartment when she added, "Have a peep at my young men too, will you: if they're awake and have a lean and hungry look, tell them they can come in and have tea."

I slid the door to and as I turned round in the corridor I came face to face with the most hideous-looking Chinaman I had ever yet set eyes upon, and I had seen a good many.

"*Yao su'mah?*" I asked abruptly. "What do you want?"

"*Mu-chin, Yao mu-chin shiao hai-tza.*" He wanted, he had said, the mother and the small children and I was wondering which would be the swiftest, surest and most noiseless way of killing him when I heard further footsteps clambering on the train from the permanent way below, and a burly figure appeared in the corridor.

"They're coming," he proclaimed breathlessly, "they're on their way. It won't be long now."

It was at that moment, I think, that my nerve cracked: the thing had become too much of a grotesque nightmare.

"*Who* are coming?" I shouted at him, overwrought and oblivious to my surroundings. "Who?"

"The British Navy are coming," was the quiet reply. "Calm yourself, laddie: though a bit informally clad, I'm Number One of the *Grasshopper* and if I were you I'd take my hands off that ruffian there because he happens to be king-pin of the chair and stretcher party and I gather he's important. Now here's the scheme . . ."

Within quarter of an hour these forerunners of the relief party had been supplemented by no less than two fully-trained doctors and nurses from the Inland Mission in Hankow escorted by an array of British naval officers and bluejackets. Emergency supplies of all kinds had arrived, and a host of Chinese were ready with the wherewithal to bear burdens of any variety or description.

The thunder of the guns and the scream of shells passing in both directions overhead grew in intensity as the party moved off in an easterly direction, where, six miles across country, two naval launches, escorted by a gun-boat, had penetrated a

creek as far as it continued to be navigable. This was an operation which, apart from actual combat with a formidable enemy
at sea, was, I suppose, as near to the heart of the British Navy as
any could be. It was carried out in a manner typical of the
Senior Service, and, I am sure, altogether in keeping with its
best traditions.

A score of bluejackets proceeded warily across the rough
countryside each carrying some unfamiliar, yet quite-at-home
youngster on his shoulders and in many cases leading another
by the hand; chatting away gaily to them as though they might
for all the world have been their own children whom they were
bringing home again after a pleasant day's excursion to the
sands. Wives and mothers, their decorum now fully restored,
rode in chairs or walked with officers of the escort and none of
them glanced more than casually over their shoulders. Between
them and the receding railway track and deserted train, moved
more slowly the end of the procession. Two baskets slung on
either end of a pole over the shoulder of a sure-footed young
Hunanese, bore Anthony and Nigel to safety, and they appeared
to be sleeping peacefully in the even motion evolved from that
half-walk-half-trot which is the gait of the practised Chinese
bearer. And then there was Kitty Forsythe, quite the bravest of
them all. She was carried on a litter borne by eight men and
flanked on either side by doctors and nurses. Every now and
then her stretcher was placed on the ground, the bearers moved
away and some special attention was given to her. I maintained
my place well to the rear of the convoy. For only once had I
essayed to walk beside her and I had noticed that her forehead
and hair were saturated, that her eyes were blinded by tears she
struggled to hold back, and there was a trickle of blood from

her lower lip which I guessed she'd bitten on, from time to time—a bit too hard.

"Hold on," I had urged, "not much further to go now . . ."

"I'm all right." She had managed to smile back. "Right as rain. You've been . . . so helpful. This is . . . awfully thrilling, isn't it?"

I had slipped back quickly again then, to the rear of the party. I could find no courage within me that might even remotely be a match for hers.

And so it was until we arrived at the narrow creek where a young and rosy-faced Lieutenant in charge of the Naval launches saw all the women and children safely housed aboard. It was significant that he turned to salute Mrs. Forsythe as she was gently hoisted over the rail and then lowered into the cabin: maybe he knew her; more likely it was just a typically naval gesture. It was, anyhow, admirably appropriate. Then he wheeled round to face me, a pair of binoculars swinging about his chest.

"Any more for the *Skylark*!" he shouted cheerfully.

"Yes," I retorted, stepping aboard. "One of your best 'shilling sicks' to Margate, please. Here—lend me those glasses."

As the gangplank was drawn in and the screws started whipping up fresh mud to the shallow surface of brown water, I looked back, through powerful lenses, across the long barren distance we had come. Dusk was just falling but I could still faintly discern the outlines of the train standing high and deserted above the embankment. A moment later the scene was obscured by a blinding red flash which was followed by a long muffled roar. As the smoke cleared I could detect that our train was now no more than a faint blur of smouldering wreckage. I lowered

222

the glasses and turned away. There had not, I reflected, been overmuch time to lose.

. . . . . .

I turned to the elder Mrs. Forsythe. It was obvious that all four of them, who had sat in silence round the table after lunch, were deeply impressed by the significance of my story.

"Your daughter-in-law and the boys," I concluded, "went on, almost immediately, to Shanghai whilst I, with others, remained for a time to sort things out in Hankow. But I had the most wonderful letter from her which I shall always cherish: and later on your son, too, wrote to me most kindly. Then presently I was posted away to the wilds of Manchuria and—you know how it is—events happen and one loses touch. So, since that evening, nearly nineteen years ago now, when they were the minutest bundles slung in baskets from either end of a bamboo pole, being borne to safety, I had not seen the twins again until I met them, by such good providence, on their way back from Church this morning."

I surveyed their massive frames, hunched in polite attention to me across the table.

"Don't worry about your mother," I urged them. "She'll come through again—all right. Perhaps now we can all feel a little more certain of that."

I glanced up at the clock, then rose and took my hostess's hand.

"Thank you: and thank you again for listening to me," I said. "For me this has been the most memorable reunion—and, may I add—a very wonderful home-coming too."

223

The old man cleared his throat, his eyebrows slightly raised. "Home-coming . . .?"

"You see, sir," I concluded, "I had a less precarious beginning than the boys. I had the advantage of everything which science had devised by the turn of the century and all the care and attention that money could provide. More precious than that, sir, I enjoyed the luxury of being born and living my earliest years, not only in the Spring magic of these lovely surroundings, but, as it strangely happens—in this very house!"

. . . . . .

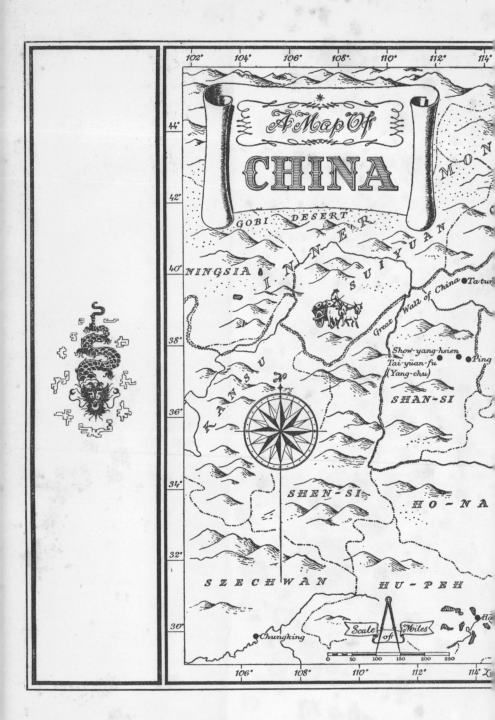

A Map Of CHINA